David
Oc

W9-ANY-921

TRAGIC ALPHABET

TRAGIC ALPHABET

Shakespeare's Drama of Language

Lawrence Danson

New Haven and London, Yale University Press, 1974

Library of Congress catalog card number: 74-79902
International standard book number: 0-300-01785-5

Designed by John O. C. McCrillis
and set in Baskerville type.
Printed in the United States of America by
The Vail-Ballou Press, Inc., Binghamton, N.Y.

Published in Great Britain, Europe, and Africa by
Yale University Press, Ltd., London.
Distributed in Latin America by Kaiman & Polon,
Inc., New York City; in Australasia and Southeast
Asia by John Wiley & Sons Australasia Pty. Ltd.,
Sydney; in India by UBS Publishers' Distributors Pvt.,
Ltd., Delhi; in Japan by John Weatherhill, Inc., Tokyo.

For

Elizabeth, Benjamin, and Joshua Danson

Thou shalt not sigh, nor hold thy stumps to heaven,
Nor wink, nor nod, nor kneel, nor make a sign,
But I of these will wrest an alphabet
And by still practice learn to know thy meaning.
                                                                    Titus Andronicus

The weight of this sad time we must obey;
Speak what we feel, not what we ought to say.
                                                                    King Lear

Contents

Preface

One of the concerns of this book (curiously, perhaps, since its subject is Shakespeare) is linguistic inadequacy, a phenomenon for which no grosser example exists than the preface to such a book. The Shakespearean critic (always an 'umble person) must apologize for his effrontery even as he is thrusting his book upon his glutted audience. There can be no excuse, but there is Shakespeare: apology and justification enough.

Equally impossible is the task of acknowledging one's intellectual indebtedness. Footnotes scarcely do the job. The author must simply bear his sense of the inexpressible debt he owes (whether acknowledged or by inadvertance omitted) to the many critics and scholars he has drawn upon. Personal obligations, though a pleasure to confess, also strain the limits of language. This book began to take shape under the teaching of Professor (now Dean) Alvin B. Kernan; but I would not want to make him responsible for anything except my gratitude, which he cannot avoid. My colleagues in the English Department of Princeton University have been generous with their advice and encouragement: to them, my thanks. And to my wife Mimi, and to Benjamin and Joshua, the book is dedicated.

I have quoted throughout from the Tudor Edition of *The Complete Works*, edited by Peter Alexander (London and Glasgow, 1951). References are to act, scene, and first line quoted; for prose passages line numbers are occasionally approximate. Parts of chapter 1 and chapter 7 have appeared, in different forms, in (respectively) *Texas Studies in Literature and Language* (published by the University of Texas Press) and *Philological Quarterly.*

I

Introduction: *Titus Andronicus*

Ben Jonson, with his career to protect in 1614, had reason to
be contemptuous of a crude old play like *Titus Andronicus*.
There were playgoers who could swear that Shakespeare's
Titus or Kyd's *The Spanish Tragedy* "are the best playes, yet";
such a one "shall passe unexpected at, heere, as a man whose
Iudgement shewes it is constant, and hath stood still, these
five and twentie, or thirtie, yeeres." [1] But if we today share a
smile at Jonson's backhanded compliment, we should do so
uneasily, for we have learned not to be complacent about
that audience whose taste for blood and bombast made possible, not only Hieronimo and Titus, but Hamlet and Lear as
well. That *Titus Andronicus* could find a responsive auditory
well into the Jacobean period is a telling fact in its favor.

It is a fact that leads immediately to a curious consideration. For this play which could elicit an audience's sympathetic
response is one that presents to us the image of a world in
which man's words go unheeded and his gestures unacknowl-
edged, a world unresponsive to his cries, demands, prayers.
The tragic world is a nightmare world; and in *Titus* the nightmare is that widely familiar one of the unutterable scream,
the unattainable release from horror through outcry or
gesture.

Now there is a relationship to be observed between these
two facts, that (on the one hand) the play found a responsive-
ness in its audience and that (on the other) the material with
which the play deals is the characters' inability, within the

---

1. Induction to *Bartholomew Fair,* in C. H. Herford and Percy and
Evelyn Simpson, *Ben Jonson,* 11 vols. (Oxford, 1925–52) 6 : 16.

world of the play, to find an adequate hearing. It is a relationship bearing upon a basic aspect of tragic theory: that things
painful to behold in life can yet give us pleasure when transmuted into art. And to find that relationship we will have to
turn to the play itself and trace its pattern of withered gestures and virtual silence.

First, however (since *Titus Andronicus* is for me, as it was
for Shakespeare, prologue to the tragedies that follow it), I
want to glance at some ways in which the situation in this
early play adumbrates a persistent Shakespearean concern
—and to show, incidentally, some of my own concerns as well.
All of Shakespeare's tragic heroes share with Titus a self-
expressive task: as they suffer greatly they must speak greatly,
their eloquence matching their pain. But everywhere, although
not so obviously as in *Titus*, the great difficulty of that task
is apparent. If we recall from *Hamlet* the perfect utterance of
"Absent thee from felicity awhile," we recall, too, the frequent communicative tangles that have preceded it, when
Hamlet fails to make himself understood by the other characters or, really, by the audience. In his intricate punning, and
in his rages when he falls "a-cursing like a very drab," Hamlet
himself is almost reduced to "inexplicable dumb shows and
noise." Similarly, we recall Lear's beautiful dream of a life
in prison with Cordelia—"We two alone will sing like birds
i' th' cage"—but also the mad ramblings on the heath, and at
the start of all, the ritual love-test that silences the communion it was meant to establish. What we watch in a
Shakespearean tragedy, then, is not only man speaking, but
man trying to speak, trying to create the language that can
denote him truly.

A presupposition here is that Shakespeare, supremely the
user of language, *thought* about the use of language, and that
he was fully self-conscious about his own strange enterprise,
the massing of words into fictive worlds. In my discussions,
then, I shall consider the tragedies not only as dramas written
in words but *about* words as well; and I shall be as much
interested in the difficulties Shakespeare's characters encounter

in their search for adequate expressive modes as in their eventual possible triumphs. But my concern will not be with words alone; it will not be a linguistic analysis in any technical sense. For Shakespeare, as a consummate man of the theater, had to conceive the art of expression as involving also movement, costume, scenery, and so on. He had to see man as *homo ludens* (in the special sense drama adds to that phrase), and to discover (in the phrase of Florio's Montaigne) that "there is no motion, nor jesture, that doth not speake."

The variety of expressive modes, the need to speak and to be understood; the great importance of the self-expressive task and its tragic precariousness: these are among the radical facts of Shakespeare's tragedies. Thus, Titus Andronicus is engaged in a definitively Shakespearean action (despite the grotesquerie of the situation) when he swears to his speechless daughter Lavinia:

> Thou shalt not sigh, nor hold thy stumps to heaven,
> Nor wink, nor nod, nor kneel, nor make a sign,
> But I of these will wrest an alphabet
> And by still practice learn to know thy meaning.
>
> [III.ii.42]

To "wrest an alphabet" from the human form and to find a language that will speak adequately of the complexities of human existence are central tasks, for Shakespeare, his characters, and his audience.

Montaigne's phrase (quoted above) comes from a passage that has a beguiling pertinence to this discussion. In it, an exuberant display of rhetorical copiousness is enlisted to prove the superiority of a language of gesture to one of words. Dazzling verbal profusion is made to express skepticism about the efficacy of words—but a skepticism which, as the passage unrolls its apparently endless bounty, ironically threatens to disprove itself in its very assertion:

> What doe we with our hands? Doe we not sue and entreate, promise and performe, call men unto us, & discharge them, bid them farewell, and be gone, threaten,

pray, beseech, deny, refuse, demaund, admire, number,
confesse, repent, feare, be ashamed, doubt, instruct, com-
maund, encite, encovrage, sweare, witnesse, accuse, con-
demne, absolve, injurie, despise, defie, despight, flatter,
aplaude, blesse, humble, mocke, reconcile, recommend,
exalt, shew-gladnes, rejoyce, complaine, waile, sorrow, discomfort, dispaire, cry-out, forbid, declare silence and
astonishment? And what not? With so great variation, and
amplifying, as if they would contend with the tongue. And
with our head, doe we not envite and call to-vs, discharge
and send away, avowe, disavowe, be-lie, welcome, honour,
worship, disdaine, demaund, direct, rejoyce, affirme, deny,
complaine, cherish, blandish, chide, yeeld, submit, brag,
boast, threaten, exhort, warrant, assure, and enquire?
What do we with our eye-lids? And with our shoulders?
To conclude, there is no motion, nor jesture, that doth not
speake, and speakes in a language, very easie, and without
any teaching to be vnderstood: nay, which is more, it is
a language common and publicke to all: whereby it fol-
loweth (seeing the varietie, and severall vse it hath from
others) that this must rather be deemed the proper and
peculier speech of humane nature.[2]

The ambivalence enacted here toward the language of words
is common to Shakespeare's time and place. That it was (on
the one hand) a period of great excitement about the possibilities of the English language is a point that needs little belabor-
ing. One could adduce a work like Richard Carew's *The Ex-
cellency of the English Tongue* (1595–96?), or the numerous
"defenses" of poetry, or encyclopedias of rhetoric like Putten-
ham's *The Arte of English Poesie* (1589). The Elizabethan
interest in translation is another measure of this excitement;
the passage I have quoted from Florio's Montaigne almost
convinces us, despite its witty disclaimer, that there is nothing words cannot do.

2. "An Apologie of Raymond Sebond," in *The Essayes* (1603), trans.
John Florio (facsimile ed., Menston, England, 1969), p. 261.

The theater, of course, had its place in all this; Thomas Heywood made it an important part of his *Apology for Actors* (1607?; published 1612) that, "our *English* tongue, which hath ben the most harsh, vneuen, and broken language of the world . . . is now by this secondary meanes of playing, continually refined, euery writer striuing in himself to adde a new florish vnto it; so that in processe . . . it is growne to a most perfect and composed language, and many excellent workes, and elaborate Poems writ in the same, that many Nations grow inamored of our tongue (before despised)." [3] And indeed, as Heywood suggests, the best proof of the Englishman's infatuation with his language comes from the arts themselves: from Spenser's immeasurably ambitious epic, to Prince Hal's intoxicated report to Poins of his anthropological field-work "with three or four loggerheads amongst three or fourscore hogsheads," the literature of the age bears everywhere the mark of its linguistic exuberance.

Less obvious, however, is the way in which all this confidence and linguistic assertiveness might imply, for the thoughtful poet, its own opposite. The mere technician would revel in his powerful new tool; the authentic discoverer, however, might feel, along with his exhilaration, the potential threat in this, as in any, great new force. Thus Shakespeare, near the end of his career, shows us in *The Tempest* the triumph of the word-magician; but still Prospero's renunciation of his art has affinities with the hysterical promise of Marlowe's earlier, damned magician, "I'll burn my books!" And in all his plays, even from the early and light *Love's Labour's Lost* (where the very subject is words, their use and abuse), Shakespeare shows his awareness of what is at best the inadequacy, at worst the real danger, in our great linguistic enterprise.

In *Titus Andronicus* (to which we now return) the latter, tragic attitude toward the possibilities for human expressiveness is most—one might say horribly—evident. For here it is

3. "Reprinted from the third edition of MDLXXXV, under the superintendence of William B. D. D. Turnbull" (London and Edinburgh, 1836), p. 160.

not a question (as it is in the passage by Montaigne) of the tongue *versus* other expressive organs; rather, the image that dominates the play (most infamously in the person of Lavinia) is of humanity tongueless and limbless, sunk in a world inimical to its fundamental need to be understood, yet still trying by every means to speak. Lavinia's plight, like much in the play, teeters on the brink of the ludicrous—for *Titus* (like *King Lear*) is a play that deals so insistently with humanity in extremis that the comic grotesque is always available to relieve us from the burden of its inordinate vision. Thus, at the beginning of Act IV, young Lucius enters fleeing from his aunt Lavinia: deprived of tongue and hands, Lavinia, by her incomprehensible gestures, can only terrify the child as she tries to calm him. Now Titus and Marcus enter and interpose for Lavinia:

> *Tit.*   Fear her not, Lucius, somewhat doth she mean.
> See, Lucius, see how much she makes of thee.
> Somewhither would she have thee go with her.
> Ah, boy, Cornelia never with more care
> Read to her sons than she hath read to thee
> Sweet poetry and Tully's Orator.
>
> [IV.i.9]

Lucius is carrying his copy of Ovid; in it Lavinia directs their attention to "the tragic tale of Philomel," and then painfully writes in the sand the names of her ravishers.

Now amidst all this pathos, the egregious touch is the reference to "Sweet poetry and Tully's Orator." For Tully's Orator is, in all probability, *Ad M. Brutum Orator,* the epistle in which Cicero depicts his ideal orator. And the reference underscores how nearly Lavinia has been reduced to the barely human, the almost monstrous: her grotesque inability to communicate sets her at the opposite pole from Cicero's orator, the man who is able to bring to bear all the distinctively human characteristics in the accomplishing of his high art. In its context, the reference might almost seem a cruel joke—but it is not meant to be one, for to the Elizabethans this matter of speaking well, of oratory, was a matter of the highest seriousness: *"Oratio* next to *Ratio,* Speech next to Reason, [is] the greatest gyft bestowed vpon mortalitie." [4] The idea ran deep: in the earliest English-language textbook of logic, Thomas Wilson's *Rule of Reason* (1551), the example given of "an undoubted true proposition" is, *"Homo est animal ratione praeditum, loquendi facultatem habens.* A man is a liuing creature endewed with reason, having aptnesse by nature to speake." [5]

We shall have to return to this question of oratory and rhetoric later; here it is only necessary to realize what it means to be deprived of the humanizing gift of speech. The image of the silenced Lavinia haunts the play. Suffering humanity is faced with an expressive imperative—to make known its pain and thus (by the act of making it known) its humanness to gods and fellow men—yet is successively deprived of its "proper and peculier speech."

It would be tedious to record all the instances of beseeching and petitioning in *Titus;* there are too many of them. It is, however, worth noting that the first disappointed petitioner is the (temporarily) conquered queen of Goths, Tamora, and that it is Titus to whom she prays for her son's life:

Stay, Roman brethren! Gracious conqueror,
Victorious Titus, rue the tears I shed,
A mother's tears in passion for her son;
And if thy sons were ever dear to thee,
O, think my son to be as dear to me.
. . . .
Thrice-noble Titus, spare my first-born son
[I.i.104, 120]

But what Tamora calls a "cruel, irreligious piety" demands the sacrifice of her son; and the only response to her entreaty

---

4. Sir Philip Sidney, "An Apologie for Poetrie," in *Elizabethan Critical Essays,* ed. G. Gregory Smith (Oxford, 1904), 1 : 182.

5. Quoted by W. S. Howell, *Logic and Rhetoric in England 1500–1700* (Princeton, N.J., 1956), p. 18.

is the announcement (in what may be Shakespeare's worst half-line), "Alarbus' limbs are lopp'd" (143). Within the same act, Titus's sons and brother kneel and beseech him to allow Mutius's burial (which, grudgingly, he does), and Titus, his sons, his brother, and Tamora plead for favor from Saturninus.

One may be tempted to say that all the succeeding instances of Titus's own inability to receive an adequate response to his entreaties arise from that first instance of his deafness to Tamora—as (to take a comparable example) one might be tempted to say that Lear's sufferings all result from his willful deafness to Cordelia's expressive silence. But that would be too narrow a view of either play. Like Lear's, Titus's punishment so far exceeds the crime that the prevailing deafness to the human voice in its cries for mercy or justice is made to seem endemic to the play's world, beyond any one man's causing. In Act II, Lavinia's mutilation takes place against the ironically gay noise of dogs and horns (II.ii.1–6); but for Aaron the Moor, "The woods are ruthless, dreadful, deaf, and dull" (II.i.128), and there Chiron and Demetrius are to "strike her home by force, if not by words" (118). As Tamora had pleaded, now Lavinia pleads:

> *Lav.* O Tamora! thou bearest a woman's face—
> *Tam.* I will not hear her speak; away with her!
> [II.iii.136]

And even as Chiron and Demetrius (offstage) rape and mutilate Lavinia, it becomes Titus's turn to plead. Aaron has arranged matters so that Titus's sons seem guilty of Bassianus's murder; and like Lavinia's plea, Titus's plea on their behalf is cut off in mid-cry:

> *Tit.* High Emperor, upon my feeble knee
> I beg this boon, with tears not lightly shed,
> That this fell fault of my accursed sons—
> Accursed if the fault be prov'd in them—
> *Sat.* If it be prov'd! You see it is apparent.
> [II.iii.288]

The need to find a satisfactory response to these interrupted pleas becomes (as the incidents of frustration mount) an overwhelming concern. Lavinia, *"her hands cut off, and her tongue cut out, and ravish'd,"* is, as we have seen, the monument that most forcefully figures this need. But we must notice, too, the response of the other Andronici to Lavinia. Marcus, for instance, is the first to encounter his mutilated niece, and he gives us one of the clearest statements of the motif:

> Shall I speak for thee? Shall I say 'tis so?
> O, that I knew thy heart, and knew the beast,
> That I might rail at him to ease my mind!
> Sorrow concealed, like an oven stopp'd,
> Doth burn the heart to cinders where it is.
>
> [II.iv.33]

Lavinia's plight, Marcus says (in one of the numerous echoes of the Ovidian tale), is worse than Philomela's:

> Fair Philomel, why she but lost her tongue,
> And in a tedious sampler sew'd her mind;
> But, lovely niece, that mean is cut from thee.
> A craftier Tereus, cousin, hast thou met. . . .

The means of expression being lost to Lavinia, the burden of expression now falls on others: "Do not draw back, for we will mourn with thee; / O, could our mourning ease thy misery!" (II.iv.56).

And on Titus himself the burden of expression falls most heavily. At the opening of Act III, we find Titus pleading with the judges and senators for his sons' lives. When his words fail, he falls upon the ground to write in dust, "My heart's deep languor and my soul's sad tears" (III.i.13). Although the tribunes will not heed Titus, "yet plead I must," and,

> Therefore I tell my sorrows to the stones;
> Who though they cannot answer my distress,
> Yet in some sort they are better than the Tribunes,
> For that they will not intercept my tale.
>
> [III.i.37]

Now Lavinia is brought before Titus. The imperious need
for relief through expression, which has already led to his
writing in dust and pleading with stones, leads now to the con-
templation of a further series of fantastic actions:

> Shall thy good uncle and thy brother Lucius
> And thou and I sit round about some fountain,
> Looking all downwards to behold our cheeks
> How they are stain'd, like meadows not yet dry,
> With miry slime left on them by a flood?
> And in the fountain shall we gaze so long,
> Till the fresh taste be taken from that clearness,
> And made a brine-pit with our bitter tears?
> Or shall we cut away our hands like thine?
> Or shall we bite our tongues, and in dumb shows
> Pass the remainder of our hateful days?
> What shall we do? Let us that have our tongues
> Plot some device of further misery
> To make us wonder'd at in time to come.
>
> [III.i.122]

Titus's final lines—"Plot some device of further misery /
To make us wonder'd at in time to come"—deserve special attention. In them is found the motivation for many of the
grotesque actions that follow. And in them, too, is found an
important nexus binding the characters' existential concerns
with the playwright's esthetic ones. To "plot some device"
can mean simply to plan a clever trick; but both "plot" and
"device" have other connotations, of a specifically artistic
and dramatic nature, which indicate that Titus's injunction
has significance for the playwright's as well as the revenger's
craft. The word *plot* is, of course, especially common in this
double sense throughout the drama of the period, and needs
no special comment here. *Device,* as Titus uses it, carries a related double sense which can yield further insights into the
relationship of playwright's craft to revenger's. According
to the *OED* (whose definitions I quote at length because they
form a relevant progression from a type of nonverbal expres-

sion to purely verbal to verbal and gestural combined), *de-vice* can mean: "8. Something artistically devised or framed; a fancifully conceived design or figure. 9. *spec.* An emblematic figure or design, *esp.* one borne or adopted by a particular person, family, etc., as a heraldic bearing, a cognizance, etc.: usually accompanied by a motto. 10. A fanciful, ingenious, or witty writing or expression, a 'conceit'. 11. Something devised or fancifully invented for dramatic representation; 'a mask played for private persons,' or the like."

In *Titus Andronicus* (as well as in the play Jonson aptly bracketed with it, *The Spanish Tragedy*—indeed, in most tragic drama from the late 1580s and the 1590s) we find these various forms of expression (the related senses of *device*) in more or less uneasy mixture. Hieronimo's "play . . . in sundry languages," with which *The Spanish Tragedy* culminates, is a device in the final sense cited from the *OED*. And through-out the play Kyd has introduced other devices that figure forth the play's central concerns. What is for our purpose most interesting to observe, is how many of Kyd's devices comprise more or lass static conceits for the difficulty Hieronimo and others find in achieving satisfaction through the use of words —as if the variety of dramatic techniques were mirroring the characters' wrestlings with the problem of expression. To cite only a few examples: an old man who has lost his son pleads for redress to a Knight Marshall who has lost *his* son; Pedrin-gano goes blithely to his death while a messenger points to an empty box that is supposed to contain a written pardon; Bel-imperia, who knows the truth of Horatio's murder, drops a message written in blood to Hieronimo—who suspects a trick (or "device" in the related sense) and fails to heed its contents.

Titus Andronicus similarly contains a series of devices that adumbrate the frustrated need to speak. The mutilated La-vinia is, as we have seen, the central such device, a conceit for the nearness of man to monster when deprived of the humaniz-ing gift of expression, and (more narrowly) an emblem for the plight of the voiceless Andronici in a now alien Rome. The responses Titus proposes—to weep all day into a fountain,

to pass their days in dumb-shows—are related devices, here
with the added implication of dramatic spectacle. A bare re-
cital of the actions that do follow will sound ludicrous unless
we recognize them for the devices they are: intentionally con-
ceited, emblematic—and each related to the same basic problem of expression needed but denied.

For instance: Titus sacrifices a hand to save his sons' lives;
thus mutilated, he and Lavinia pray to heaven—and receive
his sons' severed heads in reply. Lavinia writes the names of
her ravishers in the sand, and Titus proposes transferring the
words to more durable brass. At Titus's bidding, the Andronici
shoot petitioning arrows at the gods; and because *Terras
astraea reliquit,* Titus proposes searching for the goddess at
sea or underground. Finally there is Titus's revenge itself, in
all its elaboration (for here the sense of dramatic performance
or masque is most strong) and apparent excessiveness (involving his own and Lavinia's deaths); but of this example, where
tableau, words, and gesture combine in a culminating expressive action, we must reserve discussion until we can explore
the latter part of Titus's injunction: "Let us that have our
tongues / Plot some device of further misery / *To make us
wonder'd at in time to come.*"

Here I must acknowledge an anomaly that will in any case
have been apparent. *Titus Andronicus,* I have said, is a play
about silence, and about the inability to achieve adequate expression for overwhelming emotional needs; but the thing we
may notice before all else in it, even before its physical horrors, is its extreme, obtrusive rhetorical elaboration. But if
there is something absurd about Titus's loquacity—his endless
talking and endless elaboration about his inability to make
his cries for justice heard—the absurdity was not lost on Shakespeare. Shakespeare (as we shall see) is entirely conscious of
the disparity between Titus's rhetorical copiousness and his
ineffectuality in the realm of action, and in fact makes of it
a central dramatic motive.

For Shakespeare knows (to adapt a phrase of Jonas Barish)

not only "the pleasures," but also the "perils of rhetoric." [6] And this self-consciousness in regard to his medium points toward the very close but uneasy relationship between drama and rhetoric in his period. To the Elizabethans, indeed, orator and actor were essentially the same; in one of his additions to *The Overburian Characters,* for instance, John Webster asserts that "Whatsoever is commendable in the grave Orator, is most exquisitly perfect in ['An Excellent Actor']." Curiously, it seems to have been as much the use of action as of words which established this identity; the Overburian sketch justifies its comparison of actor and orator by noting that "by a full and significant action of the body, he [the actor] charmes our attention." [7] This apparent anomaly, that action should be the quality which links orator and actor, is taken up by Francis Bacon in his "Of Boldness":

> It is a trivial grammar-school text, but yet worthy a wise man's consideration. Question was asked of Demosthenes, *what was the chief part of an orator?* he answered, *action:* what next? *action:* what next again? *action.* He said it that knew it best, and had by nature himself no advantage in that he commended. A strange thing, that that part of an orator which is but superficial, and rather the virtue of a player, should be placed so high, above those other notable parts of invention, elocution, and the rest; nay almost alone, as if it were all in all.[8]

The commonness of the relationship is worth noticing here, but so too is Bacon's contemptuous tone. For by "action"

6. *"The Spanish Tragedy,* or The Pleasures and Perils of Rhetoric," *Stratford-upon-Avon Studies,* vol. 9 (1966).

7. *The Overburian Characters, to which is added A Wife,* ed. W. J. Paylor (Oxford, 1936), p. 76. The character of "An Excellent Actor" was added in the sixth impression, 1615; its attribution to Webster is generally accepted, and the piece is included in F. L. Lucas's edition of Webster.

8. Bacon, "Of Boldness," in *The Works,* ed. James Spedding, R. L. Ellis, and D. D. Heath (London, 1870), 6 : 401.

(that "virtue of a player") Bacon means only the particular gesture of hand and body that must accompany speech. It is a merely technical skill, the suiting of the action to the word and the word to the action that Hamlet recommends to his players; and it is a sufficiently limited notion of action to justify Bacon's contempt.

Most importantly for us, this relationship between oratory and acting, based on a rather mechanical notion of "action," indicates a real danger for the dramatist. In some of the devices we have noticed in *Titus* and *The Spanish Tragedy* the danger is apparent, for such passages tend toward the static: they are speaking pictures unnaturally situated within the frame of the surrounding action. If drama was in debt to "Tully's Orator" and the other textbooks of rhetoric that were at the heart of Elizabethan education, it was also possible that drama would perish beneath the burden of the loan. Much drama did in fact succumb: *Gorboduc,* for instance, although Philip Sidney (since he was not a playwright) could afford to luxuriate in its "stately speeches and well sounding Phrases," is dead to us because it remained rhetoric and found no really organic way to suit its words to its actions.

Inevitably, therefore, it became the superior playwright's task to broaden the notion of "action" beyond the particular gesture until it encompassed the whole play, to find the action —now in a sense closer to Aristotle's (in the *Poetics*) than to Bacon's—that would convert the raw materials of drama (including language) into the form of drama. In *Titus Andronicus* we see that conversion taking place before us. Here the struggle is in the open, the struggle to turn the language of words into the language of action, to convert (even by way of rhetoric) rhetoric itself into dramatic, and specifically tragic, form.

We see Shakespeare's recognition and handling of the problem in the paradoxical ineffectuality of the play's rhetoric— paradoxical because, however stirring it may be to the audience, it is useless to the character in achieving, in his fictive world, the results he intends. Titus has cried out to the heavens (having exhausted the world of men, of dust and stones) and, through elaborate imagery, has sought to involve the most elemental forces of nature in his lament. His words are of no avail, yet he must speak:

> If there were reason for these miseries,
> Then into limits could I bind my woes.
> When heaven doth weep, doth not the earth o'erflow?
> If the winds rage, doth not the sea wax mad,
> Threat'ning the welkin with his big-swol'n face?
> And wilt thou have a reason for this coil?
> I am the sea; hark how her [Lavinia's] sighs do blow.
> She is the weeping welkin, I the earth;
> Then must my sea be moved with her sighs;
> Then must my earth with her continual tears
> Become a deluge, overflow'd and drown'd;
> For why my bowels cannot hide her woes,
> But like a drunkard must I vomit them.
> Then give me leave; for losers will have leave
> To ease their stomachs with their bitter tongues.
> *Enter a Messenger, with two heads and a hand.*
> [III.i.220]

Here again is recognition that "Sorrow concealed, like an oven stopp'd, / Doth burn the heart to cinders where it is." But though action may be the chief part of oratory, for Titus it is the vast gap between even the most rhetorically elaborate speech and effective action which is most painfully noticeable. The stage direction that breaks off Titus's lament is one of the play's most horrifying devices for that gap. Titus's lament is compulsive: men in such extremes must speak out; but it is also, apparently, useless.

And it can be worse. For as the need to find relief through expression becomes more pressing, and as the responding rhetoric becomes more extreme and obtrusive, we find that from the heights of linguistic invention we are plunged into the nadir of madness and mad-speech. Thus Titus, having sought to ease his stomach with his bitter tongue and receiving his sons' severed heads and his own hand in response, is for a moment ominously still; Marcus prompts him: "Now is a time to storm"—but Titus's only reply is the laughter of the mad (III.i.264).

There may, however, be another way of looking at this descent into madness: the plunge may be, like Gloucester's from the cliffs at Dover, no plunge at all; it may be a mere step in an inevitable progression from lingustic elaboration to the dissolution of language itself. What is it, after all, that disturbs us about the rhetorical showpieces? Is it not that, in them, the sheer prominence of language breaks the expected bonds between words and world until we feel that the former has gained mastery over the latter? Mad-speech is, similarly, a language that has lost its connections with objective reality, words without referents in the shared world of the sane. The art of rhetoric, which can be the index of man's reason, can also, when it grows to a surfeit, be the token of madness.

The question of madness and mad-speech is crucial to an understanding of Shakespearean tragedy. We shall recur to it with *Hamlet* and *Lear* and (to a lesser extent) with other plays. Here I would point to only one aspect of the matter—the fact that madness isolates, and that mad-speech, therefore, subverts an essential function of language, the bringing together of men in the communion of a shared tongue. In *Titus Andronicus* we have already seen moments when a speaker's words reveal him locked in the privacy of his obsessions; and those moments of actual or near-madness are precisely those of the fullest, most magniloquent rhetorical elaboration. We have encountered such a moment in Titus's conceit of himself as earth and Lavinia as "weeping welkin." And we have encountered a more subtle and significant example in Act III, scene 2; it begins with Titus's promise to the silenced Lavinia that she will still somehow be heard:

> Speechless complainer, I will learn thy thought;
> In thy dumb action will I be as perfect
> As begging hermits in their holy prayers.

Thou shalt not sigh, nor hold thy stumps to heaven,
Nor wink, nor nod, nor kneel, nor make a sign,
But I of these will wrest an alphabet,
And by still practice learn to know thy meaning.

[39]

It is a noble speech in its determination that human in-
genuity can overcome the barbarity that has silenced Lavinia;
and here Titus's rhetorical copiousness is appropriate and
moving. But almost immediately the optimism is shattered:
Marcus strikes at a fly that has settled on his dish, and Titus
launches into a series of fantastic speeches that seem still to
have been reverberating in Shakespeare's mind when he came
to write *King Lear:*

> *Tit.*   Out on thee, murderer, thou kill'st my heart!
> Mine eyes are cloy'd with view of tyranny;
> A deed of death done on the innocent
> Becomes not Titus' brother. Get thee gone;
> I see thou are not for my company.
> *Marc.*   Alas, my lord, I have but kill'd a fly.
> *Tit.*   "But"! How if that fly had a father and mother?
> How would he hang his slender gilded wings,
> And buzz lamenting doings in the air!
> Poor harmless fly,
> That with his pretty buzzing melody
> Came here to make us merry! And thou hast kill'd him.

[III.ii.54]

With Marcus's explanation that "it was a black ill-favour'd
fly, / Like to the Empress' Moor," Titus swings violently
about. Now killing the fly becomes "a charitable deed," and
Titus demands,

> Give me thy knife, I will insult on him,
> Flattering myself as if it were the Moor
> Come hither purposely to poison me.
> There's for thyself, and that's for Tamora.

[71]

Titus's prosopopeia on the harmless fly, with his "lamenting
doings" and "pretty buzzing melody," is an extraordinary
thing—purposefully sentimental, beautifully realized as
poetry. And considering Titus's emotional state, one is even
able to forgive the illogic by which a murdered fly laments
his parents' bereavement. Fine. But what has become of
Lavinia in all this? And what of the effort to "wrest an
alphabet" from her gestures? The possibility of communion is
shattered as Titus wanders off in his acrid smoke of rhetoric.
At the very moment that the need for human communication
is most forcefully presented, we witness words destroying their
natural function.[9]

The nexus of characters' concerns and playwright's here becomes clearest. The playwright in the world of his craft, and
his characters in their created world, are faced with an
analogous problem: how to break out of rhetoric, that high
gift which has become a prison, and achieve the action which
will suffice? For the playwright, as I have said, that action must
be one broadly conceived, sufficient to transform the language of words into the language of drama. And how this
can be achieved is indicated by Titus's desire to "Plot some
device of further misery / To make us wonder'd at in time
to come."

The theatrical implications of the first part of Titus's lines
we have already glanced at; and we may notice that, as the
moment of Titus's revenge approaches, such double entendre
becomes more frequent: Tamora, creating a masquelike device
of her own (she is disguised as Revenge, Chiron and Demetrius
as Murder and Rape), comes to where Titus "ruminate[s]
strange plots of dire revenge" (V.ii.6); Titus plans to "o'er-
reach them in their own devices" (V.ii.143); and when he has
killed Chiron and Demetrius, he announces as the next part
of his plan that "I will play the cook" (V.ii.205). Through

9. The authenticity of the scene has been questioned, especially on the
grounds that the next scene begins with the reentry of characters who
exit at the end of this scene. The scene may be a later addition, but
I see no reason to attribute it to any hand other than Shakespeare's.

such suggestions of a play-within-a-play, the world of reality and the world of the stage begin to merge in a way that animates Ralegh's poetic cliché, "Thus march we playing to our latest rest, / Only we die in earnest; that's no jest." In *Titus Andronicus* the earnest of death becomes inextricably bound up with the jest of playing.

But in what way can the play's "plot of dire revenge," which includes the deaths of Lavinia and Titus himself, satisfy the demand that it be a plot "To make us wonder'd at in time to come"? Again we must attend to a special sense of Titus's language. According to J. V. Cunningham, the word *wonder* (the normal translation of the Latin *admiratio*), in a tradition descending from Aristotle, was closely associated with the particular emotion supposed to derive from tragedy. "The effect of astonishment or wonder is the natural correlative of unusual diction, as it is of the unusual event," Cunningham writes; in particular, "the high style, the forceful, the grand— the style of Demosthenes and Aeschylus—will evoke that wonder which is akin to fear, and will be especially appropriate to tragedy." [10]

But we have already seen that *Titus Andronicus* carries with it, just as it is exploiting the language of wonder, the recognition that even the most unusual diction and the highest style will not suffice: action, and that a very special action, must animate the otherwise imprisoning rhetoric. And the action that will not only fit but transform the words is death: for the Elizabethan tragedian, death is what can provoke "wonder" in time to come. J. V. Cunningham explains:

> The tragic fact is death. Even the most natural death has in it a radical violence, for it is a transition from this life to something by definition quite otherwise; and however much it may be expected, it is in its moment of incidence sudden, for it comes as the thief in the night, you know not the day nor the hour. Hence the characteristics of suddenness and violence which are attached to death in tragedy may be viewed as artistic heightenings of

10. *Woe or Wonder* (Denver and Toronto, 1951), p. 73.

the essential character of death: the unnaturalness of the tragic event is only pointed and emphasized by the unnatural precipitancy of its accomplishment.[11]

In this play, when words have done their uttermost and failed, Titus breaks through the barriers of incommunicability with the gesture which, because it is the gesture most provocative of wonder, is definitive of Elizabethan and Jacobean tragedy. He takes the final step from rhetoric through madness to death.

It may seem an anticlimax to conclude this introductory discussion with the mere fact of death, especially since everyone knows (even those who have never read or seen the play) that *Titus Andronicus* is a "revenge tragedy"—and hence, by definition, that its finale must be, in every sense, deadly. But the next play to which I will turn is also a revenge tragedy: and merely to put together the names of *Titus Andronicus* and *Hamlet* suggests the need for a more searching examination of the related questions of death and revenge than the circularity that only tells us you can't have one without the other. In the discussion of *Hamlet* I will show more fully how Shakespeare ties the convention of revenge to that imperious need for self-expression we see dramatized in *Titus*. But even at this point a beginning can be made.

Revenge, I would suggest, is only one of the various routes by which Shakespeare approached his real destination, the culminating action that may bring "wonder" out of rhetoric in time to come. Through his extended pursuit of revenge, the tragic hero plays out the ritualization of death which permits his tragedy to conclude with the expressiveness of a *consummatum est*. The sense of something attained after great travail, something at once fearful and wondrous, is the dramatic solution to a problem that haunts much of Renaissance literature, be it sonnet or tragedy—the problem (to use Spenser's word) of mutability. The resolution in death is necessary to assure

11. Ibid., p. 59.

the sort of enduring memorial Titus and his creator seek, and is an integral part of the play's expressive form.

The demand for permanence explains a function of those somewhat dazed survivors who preside over the tragic close, the Horatios and Edgars, with their promise to remember the events and report them "aright / To the unsatisfied." In *Titus*, it is true, the remaining Andronici are annoyingly wordy, a fact perhaps forgivable under the circumstances: they have been effectually voiceless in Rome long enough. Still, this is a long way from the more honest ending of *King Lear*, its bathetically simple "Speak what we feel, not what we ought to say," with its recognition that not all the words in the world can balance the weight of the action we have just witnessed. Shakespeare's great tragedies—whether of revenge, blood, or tragedy pure—culminate, like their important precursor *Titus Andronicus*, in the acting out of death; and the rest is, necessarily, silence.

2

Hamlet

"Speak to it. . . . It would be spoke to. . . . By heaven I charge thee, speak. . . . Speak to me. . . . O, Speak!" The word beats like a bell throughout the first scene of *Hamlet,* introducing (if obliquely) one of the play's central concerns even before we meet the prince. True, there are special difficulties involved in communicating with a ghost—the protocol is obscure at best, and it is understandable that the men on watch should be confused—but the problem of *speaking* extends far beyond that special case in the course of the play. Misunderstandings are among that most frequent phenomena in *Hamlet:* Hamlet cannot or will not understand the language of the court, and the court, for its part, makes a desperate (and unsuccessful) attempt to understand the wild and whirling words of its prince. There is hardly a character with whom Hamlet does not become involved in a linguistic contretemps: Claudius and Gertrude have to remind him of (among other things) the proper kinship terms; Polonius, Rosencrantz, and Guildenstern—the interpreters Claudius sends to Hamlet—do not understand him; Ophelia does not understand his mad speeches and finally becomes, herself, "A document in madness"; while Osric and the Grave-digger (in their different ways) turn the tables on Hamlet and make *him* confess that "equivocation will undo us."

And the problem is not only verbal. The verbal difficulties mirror difficulties that exist in the realm of action—in the realm of what we might call gestural expression. Hamlet has a task to perform, a task real and deadly, but one also with a clearly symbolic dimension; his revenge must express a certain relationship to his dead father and to Claudius, to the state, to justice human and divine, and Hamlet finds that the acting of it becomes increasingly difficult as the incitements to it become more pressing. As it becomes difficult to say anything simply and directly in *Hamlet,* so it becomes difficult to do anything. And again the problem afflicts not only Hamlet but all who are involved with him: Claudius and those lesser beings "mortised and adjoined" to him are similarly driven to greater and greater indirections to find their directions out. The rottenness in Denmark has attacked the very roots of society—the symbolic systems which enable the primary social act, verbal and gestural expression.

The first instance of the problem suggests its dimensions and its cause. Marcellus and Bernardo have been unable to make the ghost speak; with a touching faith they have now called in a specialist: "Thou art a scholar; speak to it, Horatio" (I.i.42). But even Horatio is ill-equipped to break through the impasse in communication. He barrages the voiceless ghost with exhortation and finally, in frustration, calls for force; they strike at it with their partisans only to realize, "We do it wrong, being so majestical, / To offer it the show of violence" (I.i.143). Horatio, Bernardo, and Marcellus are, of course, the wrong men to deal with the ghost:

> Let us impart what we have seen to-night
> Unto young Hamlet; for, upon my life,
> This spirit, dumb to us, will speak to him.
>
> [I.i.169]

But they lack more than the proper relationship. They lack the language (words) and the other means (gestures, and words and gestures ordered as ritual) that would make communication possible. They are ignorant of protocol, confused about the sort of ceremony to use—here in the night, on the battlements, amidst the "posthaste and romage" of wartime—when addressing "the king / That was and is the question of these wars." The ghost, that is to say, is a wholly new element, un-

dreamed of in their philosophy; it is an anomaly, and there is
no customary language, no ritual, for dealing with it.

Even *before* we see the ghost we may find indications that
the problem in Denmark involves the failure of ritual. The
very first words of the play are an inversion of ceremonial
order:

> *Bev.* Who's there?
> *Fran.* Nay, answer me. Stand and unfold yourself.

And the men on guard, it appears, do not even know what it
is they are guarding against—only that it is something extraordinary. "Good now, sit down, and tell me, he that knows,"
Marcellus asks,

> Why this same strict and most observant watch
> So nightly toils the subject of the land;
> And why such daily cast of brazen cannon,
> And foreign mart for implements of war;
> Why such impress of shipwrights, whose sore task
> Does not divide the Sunday from the week;
> What might be toward, that this sweaty haste
> Doth make the night joint-labourer with the day:
> Who is't that can inform me?
>
> > [I.i.70]

The dissolving of difference between Sunday and the rest of
the week, and between night and day, are small touches, but
they are of a piece with the other "strange eruptions"—of
which the ghost is the strangest—that have deprived the men
of the certainties of custom and ceremonial. In scene 4, when
Hamlet joins the watch, the men question him, not only about
the ghost, but about the customs of King Claudius as well.
Despite "kettledrum and trumpet," even Claudius fails to
make himself understood; even the rituals of the king fail to
communicate their meanings.[1]

---

1. The influence here of Francis Fergusson's *The Idea of a Theater*
(Princeton, N.J., 1949) will be obvious to any reader of that seminal work.
In much that follows I am also indebted to John Holloway's *The Story*

In this context it is worth noting that the ghost, in speaking to Hamlet, dwells especially on the rituals that were denied him; he was

> Cut off even in the blossoms of my sin,
> Unhous'led, disappointed, unanel'd;
> No reck'ning made, but sent to my account
> With all my imperfections on my head.
> [I.v.76]

The murder was "most foul, strange, and unnatural"—and it receives this triple emphasis presumably because of the many social bonds it canceled: it was both fratricide and political assassination, and it followed acts of adultery and incest. Now the ghost must "walk the night" until "the foul crimes . . . Are burnt and purg'd away" (I.v.12).

The murder of old Hamlet is the first of the "maimed rites" in the play; others follow, especially in matters of death and interment. Polonius and Ophelia both receive "hugger-mugger" burials, and the series ends only with the play's bloody final scene. Laertes, with his bold complaints to Claudius about his father's

> means of death, his obscure funeral—
> No trophy, sword, nor hatchment, o'er his bones,
> No noble rite nor formal ostentation—
> [IV.v.209]

and his rant (as Hamlet calls it) over Ophelia's curtailed funeral, is most blatant in expressing his displeasure at the absence of the old expressive modes. But Hamlet, whose vision is deeper and whose denunciation is more subtle, sees what Laertes cannot, that the old terms of "honor"—the old rituals and (as we shall see) language itself—have become rotten and will no longer serve. The murder of old Hamlet and his reappearance in ghostly form introduce a fatal anomaly that

---

of the Night (Lincoln, Neb., 1961); cf., for instance, pp. 31–33 on "maimed rites."

destroys ritual observance and makes the demand for a new ritual that can accommodate it. The injunction to Hamlet to revenge includes the implicit demand for a new, expressive language.

When we turn from the battlements to the court we find the anomaly embodied in Hamlet himself. Amidst the celebrants of a marriage and a coronation, the prince sits silently apart, mourning a death and a usurpation. For Claudius this stark anomaly is intolerable, and his language reflects his method of dealing with it. The oxymorons of his opening speech are a desperate gambit, an attempt to make language swallow up irreconcilable differences:

> Therefore our sometime sister, now our queen . . .
> Have we, as 'twere with a defeated joy,
> With an auspicious and a dropping eye,
> With mirth in funeral, and with dirge in marriage,
> In equal scale weighing delight and dole,
> Taken to wife.
>
> [I.ii.8, 10]

But this weighing is a mere trick: the words alone balance and cancel each other out. Still, the trick might work; the courtiers, after all, have in their "better wisdoms . . . freely gone with this affair along." Only Hamlet is there to remind them of a reality not so easily manipulated.

If Claudius's mode is the oxymoron, Hamlet's is the pun. One man balances words to cancel out their antithetical meanings, while the other overbalances words *with* meanings. The pun thus typifies Hamlet's role throughout the play: it is the linguistic confrontation that precedes the physical. Claudius greets Hamlet as "my cousin Hamlet, and my son," but Hamlet responds (aside), "A little more than kin, and less than kind" (I.ii.64, 65)—informing us that Claudius's double kinship is (through the pun on "kind") both unnatural and ungracious, not at all of Hamlet's kind. "How is it that the clouds still hang on you," asks Claudius; and in Hamlet's reply—"Not so my lord; I am too much in the sun" (66, 67)—the sunshine of royal attention and the too-much sonship of double paternity become a distaste for life itself (the condition of being in the sun). "Thou know'st 'tis common—all that lives must die," says Gertrude (showing a touch of the Claudian manner in her facile balancing of *lives* with *die*): "Aye, madam, it is common," comes Hamlet's reply (72, 74), but now the word *common* is loaded with meanings that quite reverse the ameliorating effects of the oxymoron. Hamlet's punning carries with it the demand that words receive their full freight of meaning, and it is a demand that dooms to defeat Claudius's wordy attempts at compromise.[2]

An "exchange of complementary values" is the essential act of social existence. At the linguistic level, "there must be a certain equivalence between the symbols used by the addresser and those known and interpreted by the addressee," [3] to assure the success of any speech event. But at the opening of *Hamlet* (as the exchanges between Hamlet and Claudius and Gertrude show), the absence of "complementary values," of equivalent symbols, is indeed remarkable. The one word *common* conveys ideas so widely different to two speakers as to suggest that it is really two separate words. And there is no equivalence in the use of such vital symbols as *mother, father, uncle, nephew,* and *son.* Claudius's oxymoronic mode is an attempt to enforce the illusion that the symbols are univocal, while Hamlet's puns expose the equivocation that has invaded each.

So it is, too, in the other, gestural language of social transactions. "My lord, I came to see your father's funeral" (I.ii.176),

2. Sigurd Burckhardt defines a pun as "the creation of a semantic identity between words whose phonetic identity is, for ordinary language, the merest coincidence. That is to say, it is an act of verbal violence, designed to tear the close bond between a word and its meaning." The pun, he continues, "gives the lie direct to the social convention which is language. . . . It denies the meaningfulness of words and so calls into question the genuineness of the linguistic currency on which the social order depends." See Burckhardt, *Shakespearean Meanings* (Princeton, N.J., 1968), pp. 24–25.

3. Roman Jakobson and Morris Halle, *Fundamentals of Language* (The Hague, 1956), p. 62.

Horatio tells Hamlet, but even a "funeral" is now an ambiguous symbol: "I prithee do not mock me, fellow student;
I think it was to see my mother's wedding." In the midst of
the celebrating court, Hamlet's very dress and demeanor—his
"nighted colour" and "vailed lids"—are a sort of silent pun,
loading the values of "funeral" onto those of "marriage." Later
in the play, when we see Hamlet baiting Polonius—

> What do you read, my lord?
> *Ham.*   Words, words, words.
> *Pol.*   What is the matter, my lord?
> *Ham.*   Between who?
> *Pol.*   I mean, the matter that you read, my lord—
> [II.ii.190]

we will be seeing nothing different in kind from what our first
glimpse of Hamlet has already revealed. Hamlet cannot, or
will not, understand the language of the court—a language
which (as Hamlet shows Polonius in the matter of the shape-
shifting cloud) has lost its necessary relationship to a world
it no longer adequately describes.

Hamlet's puns continually probe a structural flaw in the
edifice of Denmark, threatening to bring the building down
on all their heads. He consistently brings together the bal-
anced opposites of the Claudian oxymoron and pressurizes
the contradiction to the breaking point. Closely related to his
technique of aggressive punning is the use he makes of the
syllogism. It is not sufficient that the king and queen should be
(as in his parody of the Claudian manner he calls them) "my
uncle-father and aunt-mother" (II.ii.372); by syllogistic reason-
ing Hamlet arrives at the reductio ad absurdam where the king
is simply "dear mother"—since "father and mother is man and
wife; man and wife is one flesh; and so, my mother" (IV.iii.49).

As a Wittenberg man, Hamlet knows the central importance
of the syllogism as a tool of traditional (that is, scholastic)
philosophy. But here, in using the syllogism to expose a false,
absurd situation, he sounds more like the skeptical Francis
than like the scholastic Friar Bacon. In his critique of the

"idols of the market-place," Francis Bacon was to denounce the errors which arise when the language we use fails to correspond to the truth of things-behind-language. And the syllogism would be a special point of Bacon's attack; as his case has been put by a modern historian: "The syllogism consists of propositions; and propositions consist of words; and words express concepts. Thus, if the concepts are confused and if they are the result of over-hasty abstractions, nothing which is built on them is secure." [4] What Hamlet shows by his use of the syllogism is that nothing secure can rest on the falsehood that masquerades as the royal order of Denmark.

From Claudius's point of view, however, the syllogism is simply mad: its logic is part of Hamlet's "antic disposition." Sane men know, after all, that "man and wife is one flesh" only in a metaphoric or symbolic sense; they know that only a madman would look for literal truth in linguistic conventions. And Claudius is right that such "madness in great ones must not unwatched go" (III.i.end). For the madman, precisely because he does not accept society's compromises and because he explores its conventions for meanings they cannot bear, exposes the flaws which "normal" society keeps hidden. Hamlet's wordplay, "pregnant" as it is with matters normally left undisclosed, brings to light things which (as Polonius says) "reason and sanity could not so prosperously be delivered of" (II.ii.208). Hamlet's very language—a language that is a continual probing *of* language—brings the conventions and the compromises inexorably to view.

And not only Hamlet's: the threat that madness, and mad-speech, poses to the state is shown in Ophelia too. (For, as I have already said, Hamlet's problem becomes the problem of all who are associated with him. The distance between reality and the language that ostensibly describes it in Denmark, that builds equivocation into that language and leaves Hamlet speaking his antic wordplay, leaves Ophelia, too, speaking madly.) The disorder of Ophelia's speech—its departure from

4. Frederick Copleston, S. J., *A History of Philosophy* (1953; reprinted Garden City, N.J., 1963), vol. 3, pt. 2, p. 112.

the intelligible norm—is even more significant, and threatening, than its actual content. A gentleman says of her:

> She speaks much of her father; says she hears
> There's tricks i' th' world, and hems, and beats her heart;
> Spurns enviously at straws; speaks things in doubt,
> That carry but half sense. Her speech is nothing,
> Yet the unshaped use of it doth move
> The hearers to collection; they yawn at it,
> And botch the words up fit to their own thoughts;
> Which, as her winks and nods and gestures yield them,
> Indeed would make one think there might be thought,
> Though nothing sure, yet much unhappily.
>
> [IV.v.4]

Here is the genius of great grief: Ophelia, no longer able to contain or express her experience within the bounds of "normal" behavior, finds in the virtual silence of madness the most effective, and for Claudius the most damning, speech of all. Any charges against Claudius, rationally delivered, could be rationally answered—as Claudius does indeed answer Laertes. But the charge that comes from the realm of madness is too sweeping; its very mode implies that the ordinary language is itself being condemned, and will not serve in reply.

Now no one has ever suggested (as far as I know) that Ophelia is only shamming; she has no choice about the way she speaks. But Hamlet is another matter and, even without solving the red herring of his real versus his feigned madness, we must agree that Hamlet's choice of language needs some further explanation. Most of the rest of the court sees nothing wrong with the ordinary expressive modes; Gertrude, for instance, sees nothing wrong with her use of the word *common*. Why then does Hamlet, even before the ghost appears to him, reject the language of the court, and with it the compromises that would assure a smooth social functioning? Why must the expression he seeks (which, after the ghost's appearance, will become identified with his revenge) be found outside the conventional modes available?

Lucien Goldmann defines "two essential characteristics of tragic man" which may be applied as well to our Shakespearean hero as to the Racinian heroes he discusses: "the first is that he makes [an] exclusive and absolute demand for impossible values; and the second is that, as a result of this, his demand is for 'all or nothing,' and he is totally indifferent to degrees and approximations, and to any concept containing the idea of relativity." [5] The self-negating oxymorons of Claudian rhetoric, disguising actual conflict under a show of verbal concord, reflect the sort of condition this absolutist man must find intolerable. Hamlet's disgust with the equivocal language—both words and rituals—of the Danish court leads him to his "all or nothing" attitude toward all language and ritual.

Equivocation—the conflict between the reality Hamlet perceives and the language used to describe that reality—has made all expression a matter of mere seeming, and Hamlet knows not seems. His rejection of the Claudian language extends to a rejection of all the symbolic systems that can denote a man. Thus, even his own punning (both verbal and silent) is inadequate: Hamlet chooses "nothing" since he cannot have "all":

> 'Tis not alone my inky cloak, good mother,
> Nor customary suits of silent black,
> Nor windy suspiration of forc'd breath,
> No, nor the fruitful river in the eye,
> Nor the dejected haviour in the visage,
> Together with all forms, moods, shapes of grief,
> That can denote me truly. These, indeed, seem;
> For they are actions that a man might play;
> But I have that within which passes show—
> These but the trappings and the suits of woe.
>
> [I.ii.77]

In an ambiguous world, where all is but seeming, and hence misinterpretation, no symbol is successful. The absolutist

5. *The Hidden God*, trans. Philip Thody (New York, 1964), p. 63.

Hamlet finds nothing that can denote him truly, and is driven back to the only place where indubitable truth can reside, to the self: "But I have that within which passes show."

Hamlet's insistence upon an inner essence of truth is both noble and peculiarly jejune; it is the youthful nobility which refuses to compromise between the self and the world. For such a man, the self has a value independent of its suits and trappings, and he demands that it be prized and satisfied without regard to that accidental matter, the body, which happens to go with it. There is a poem by John Donne which wittily exposes the inevitable defeat of such youthful idealism. In "The Blossome," Donne takes quite literally the duality of mind and body; and, as he is about to leave for a libertine visit to London, he addresses the heart which would stay behind in faithfulness to a denying mistress:

> Well then, stay here; but know,
>   When thou hast stayd and done thy most;
> A naked thinking heart, that makes no show,
> Is to a woman, but a kinde of Ghost;
> How shall shee know my heart; or having none,
>   Know thee for one?
> Practice may make her know some other part,
> But take my word, shee doth not know a Heart.[6]

"A naked thinking heart, that makes no show" (or: "that within which passes show"): it cannot be; it is a mere immanence (a "Ghost") needing a bodying forth in expressive action. As Hamlet tries to come to terms with the need for body and action, he shows a bitterness not unlike Donne's ("Practice may make her know some other part"); for a while in Hamlet's play, the only expressive action that seems possible is "lust in action." Hamlet's frequent expressions of sexual disgust project, in part, his feeling that the soul is raped in its commerce with the world. To speak or act in a world where all speech and action are equivocal seeming is,

6. *The Poems of John Donne*, ed. Sir Herbert Grierson (London, 1933), p. 54.

for Hamlet, both perilous and demeaning, a kind of whoring.

The whole vexed question of Hamlet's delay ought, I believe, to be considered in light of this dilemma. To a man alienated from his society's most basic symbolic modes, who finds all speech and action mere seeming and hypocritical playing, comes an imperious demand to speak and act—to express himself in deed his father's son. The ghost's stress upon ritual modes indicates that the expression demanded must not be just "a kind of wild justice," but an expression ordered and meaningful. Hamlet's difficulties at the linguistic level—his puns and "antic disposition," the lack of commensurate values between him and the rest of the court—are reflected in his difficulties at the level of action. Like Titus Andronicus, Hamlet is confronted with the expressive imperative; and the demanded expression, the act of revenge, must be an unequivocal gesture in a world where all gesture has become equivocal seeming. Hamlet must satisfy not only his dead father's needs, but also his own deepest need to be denoted truly.

The problems of expression which confront Hamlet, as I have so far discussed them, are peculiar to his world—to the Denmark constituted in murder, usurpation, incest, and adultery. But there is a further problem revealed in the course of the play, related to these but central, not only for Hamlet, but for tragic man generally. It is most fully enunciated, appropriately enough, by that tragedian of the city, the Player-King. It is the problem of time, or history, and of expression-in-time. Briefly, how can one speak or act (truly) in a world where each succeeding moment gives the last the lie, where our words are no sooner uttered than they are relegated to a discredited past and (like Achilles racing the inexorable tortoise) can never overtake the truth of the passing moment? In "The Murder of Gonzago," the Player-Queen protests that she will never remarry after her husband's death; to which he replies, in lines worth quoting extensively:

> I do believe you think what now you speak;
> But what we do determine oft we break.

Purpose is but the slave to memory,
Of violent birth, but poor validity;
Which now, the fruit unripe, sticks on the tree;
But fall unshaken when they mellow be.
Most necessary 'tis that we forget
To pay ourselves what to ourselves is debt.
What to ourselves in passion we propose,
The passion ending, doth the purpose lose.
The violence of either grief or joy
Their own enactures with themselves destroy.
Where joy most revels grief doth most lament;
Grief joys, joy grieves, on slender accident.
This world is not for aye; nor 'tis not strange
That even our loves should with our fortunes change. . . .
But, orderly to end where I begun,
Our wills and fates do so contrary run
That our devices still are overthrown;
Our thoughts are ours, their ends none of our own.
                                    [III.ii.181, 205]

The Player-King does not question his wife's sincerity: the
irrelevance of sincerity is part of the problem. He questions,
rather, the validity of any assertion of purpose made in a
world where (to quote a more pithy tragic figure) thoughts are
the slaves of life and life is time's fool. Even where thought
and expression are in tune with each other, the inevitable
movement of time ("fate") makes a liar of our "wills." In
this world of constant process, "Our thoughts are ours, their
ends none of our own."

Inexorably moving time is the discreditor of all purpose and
action: it is the primary equivocator, and for the man who
despises all seeming it raises hypocrisy to the level of a universal condition. Claudius, who knows and accepts the conditions of this world as fully as Hamlet knows and rejects them,
is in accord with the Player-King on this point. Claudius has
been trying to win over Laertes; and he knows that Laertes
(whose expressions of love for Polonius and determination to

be revenged are made with "emphasis" enough) still may be, as Claudius puts it, "Like the painting of a sorrow, / A face without a heart" (IV.vii.108). For Laertes's determination, like that of the Player-Queen, is the slave of time: "I know," Claudius says, that

> love is begun by time,
> And that I see, in passages of proof,
> Time qualifies the spark and fire of it.
> There lives within the very flame of love
> A kind of wick or snuff that will abate it;
> And nothing is at a like goodness still;
> For goodness, growing to a pleurisy,
> Dies in his own too much.
> [IV.vii.111]

Claudius, like the Player-King, does not doubt the intention: he is simply stating a general law, and it is the very absoluteness which makes it so terrible. His crafty answer to the problem of action-in-time is really no answer at all, but mere accommodation; it is simply a *carpe diem* which avoids the problem:

> That we would do,
> We should do when we would; for this 'would' changes,
> And hath abatements and delays as many
> As there are tongues, are hands, are accidents. . . .
> [IV.vii.118]

Laertes can show himself indeed his father's son by getting rid of Hamlet the nearest way. And Claudius's incitement to immediate action sounds as though it might do as a prescription for Hamlet as well, whose own task is mirrored by Laertes's. Claudius's advice would make either man an effective killer— but it would still leave them (what Hamlet refuses to be) the fools of time.

The problem of time's discrediting effects upon human actions and intentions is what makes Hamlet's "To be, or not to be" soliloquy eternal dilemma rather than fulfilled dialectic.

Faced with the uncertainty of any action, an uncertainty that
extends even to the afterlife, Hamlet, too, finds the "wick or
snuff" of which Claudius speaks: "Thus conscience"—by
which Hamlet means, I take it, not only scruples but all
thoughts concerning the future—

> does make cowards of us all;
> And thus the native hue of resolution
> Is sicklied o'er with the pale cast of thought,
> And enterprises of great pitch and moment,
> With this regard, their currents turn awry
> And lose the name of action.—
>
> [III.i.83]

Both the Player-King and Claudius discuss the temporal
dilemma in regard to love; here, Hamlet's reflections are
broken off as he catches sight of Ophelia. In the final act,
Hamlet will declare, "I loved Ophelia," but at the midway
point of his play the distressing thought that what-we-are-now
is not what-we-will-become makes love seem only one more
hypocrisy in a world of hypocrisy:

> *Oph.* My lord, I have remembrances of yours
> That I have longed long to re-deliver.
> I pray you now receive them.
> *Ham.* No, not I;
> I never gave you ought.
>
> [III.i.93]

For the gestures of yesterday are false today.

> *Ham.* I did love you once.
> *Oph.* Indeed, my lord, you made me believe so.
> *Ham.* You should not have believ'd me; for virtue
> cannot so inoculate our old stock but we shall relish
> of it. I loved you not.
> *Oph.* I was the more deceived.
>
> [III.i.115]

The only way out of the dilemma of action falsified in the
acting is to remove oneself somehow from the mortal condi-

tion: "Get thee to a nunnery. Why wouldst thou be a breeder of sinners?"

Ophelia is not only Hamlet's victim; in her limited way, she faces the same difficulties which cause him to victimize her. She, too, lives in a world of hypocritical seeming, erected (in her case) into the self-serving morality of Polonius's and Laertes's admonitions. Laertes warns her not to trust Hamlet's expressions of love, and one of the reasons he gives is that same simple reason Hamlet (with self-mocking bitterness) also gives —man is subject to time:

> For nature crescent does not grow alone
> In thews and bulk, but as this temple waxes,
> The inward service of the mind and soul
> Grows wide withal. Perhaps he loves you now. . . .
> [I.iii.11]

Polonius adds the limbs and outward flourishes to Laertes's lesson, in words recalled later by Claudius's speech:

> These blazes, daughter,
> Giving more light than heat—extinct in both,
> Even in their promise, as it is a-making—
> You must not take for fire.
> [I.iii.117]

(Claudius says, "There lives within the very flame of love / A kind of wick or snuff.") Even as it is spoken, according to Polonius, the word becomes false. And Hamlet, for the greater part of his play, would have to give his bitter assent: only silence (and inaction) can be true to that which is within.

The Polonii are concerned in a practical manner with the problem of time and growth, that man changes and therefore will be false. Hamlet takes the question the necessary one step further; man *dies,* and his death is the ultimate change that makes liars of us all. The graveyard, with Yorick's skull, is to Hamlet a most powerful symbol; it is, at least for a time, his proof that all action contains a principle of obsolescence. Alexander's world-conquering gestures are rendered as meaningless by the grave as Yorick's gibes and gambols.

Death proves that all our words and deeds are as transient, and thus ultimately false, as a lady's cosmetics: "Now get you to my lady's chamber, and tell her, let her paint an inch thick, to this favour she must come" (V.i.189). Horatio's comment, " 'Twere to consider too curiously to consider so," is a counsel of simple sanity, for Hamlet's consideration would make all "enterprises . . . their currents turn awry / And lose the name of action." But Hamlet, who has seen and considered too much to turn away now, will have to achieve his expressive action, not with eyes averted from the skull, but with the fact of death integrated in the gesture he will make.

The arrival of the players in Act II, scene 2 gathers to a focus many of the apparently disparate thematic concerns of *Hamlet;* most immediately, the coming of the players bears upon the problem of expression in a world of seeming. For these players, unlike others at Elsinore, confess their profession proudly; they are very much experts in seeming, bringing with them the gossip of the green room and merging into one complex image Hamlet's Denmark and Shakespeare's Globe Theater. Because they are actors, they have a concern for rhetoric and gesture: their very presence thus serves to remind us of the difficulty men have had at Elsinore in finding a language with which to speak to the ghost and to each other. We have been watching a king (Claudius) play his very difficult role, and have seen the difficulty of that role vastly increased by the prince's rejection of all seeming and playing. Now the prince exclaims, "He that plays the king shall be welcome" (II.ii.317).

The scene in which the players make their entrance has already acquainted us with a variety of uses for playing. Polonius has proposed a solution to the problem of Hamlet's madness, and in the process has been cautioned to speak "more matter with less art" (II.ii.95). "Madam, I swear I use no art at all," the artful Polonius responds, and then proposes, as a means for getting at the truth, an improvisation with himself and Claudius as hidden audience, and with his daughter as ingénue to Hamlet's unsuspecting romantic lead. Hamlet then treats Polonius to a private show of his feigned madness—a difficult play full of allusions and puns which seems to Polonius "pregnant" with a meaning "which reason and sanity could not so prosperously be delivered of." Polonius fails to recognize the madness as acting, but he does see a "method" in it. Finally, Rosencrantz and Guildenstern, playing the parts given them by Claudius, also use seeming to find out a truth and are met in turn with a seeming (Hamlet's) which may well be truth.

The arrival of the players at this point breaks through the tangle of involved wordplay, apparent irrelevance, and politic dissembling. Hamlet's greeting to them is warm, with a controlled excitement which seems to come from what Bradley calls "the true Hamlet, the Hamlet of the days before his father's death." [7] Perhaps Hamlet already sees in them a form of release from his noncommunicative tangle: his greeting rushes directly on to a hope: "We'll have a speech straight. Come, give us a taste of your quality; come, a passionate speech" (II.ii.425).

Robert J. Nelson, writing of the convention in general, has said that, "The play within a play is the theater reflecting on itself, on its own paradoxical seeming." [8] The Player's speech about Pyrrhus, Priam, and Hecuba is, as it were, merely a curtain raiser to the more elaborate "The Murder of Gonzago" in Act III; but it is a true play-within-a-play in providing, to paraphrase Professor Nelson, a reflection of the play *Hamlet*'s paradoxical seeming, and it is worth pausing over. Polonius finds it too long, but Hamlet is both moved and perplexed by it—by the speech itself and by the circumstances of its delivery. The Player's speech, as we shall see, brings to consciousness for Hamlet the nexus of ideas: playing-sincerity-expression-revenge.

7. *Shakespearean Tragedy* (London, 1904), p. 133.
8. *Play Within a Play* (New Haven, 1958), p. 10. The theatrical self-consciousness of *Hamlet,* and of Hamlet, has intrigued many of the play's commentators. The indispensable general study is Anne Righter's *Shakespeare and the Idea of the Play* (London, 1962).

One "reflection" is succinctly recognized in Harry Levin's analysis of the Player's speech:

> To the observer who is painfully learning the distinction between *seems* and *is,* the hideous pangs of the Trojan Queen are the mirrored distortions of Gertrude's regal insincerities. The "damn'd defeat" of Priam, reminding Hamlet of his father, prompts him to renounce his hitherto passive role, to soliloquize on the Player's example, and finally to evolve his plan of action.[9]

What Hamlet sees, that is to say, is in part the murder of a father—a murder recounted in a high heroical vein which is, in itself, a painful reminder of his own lack of heroism. But the mirror a play holds up to nature—which in the case of a play-*within*-a-play means the "nature" of the containing play —has curious properties, not the least of which is its ability to reflect more than one scene or set of images simultaneously.

Thus we need not be unduly surprised by a second "reflection" found in the Player's speech—a reflection which shows Hamlet's form in that of the father-murderer Pyrrhus. Here is the picture of Pyrrhus at the instant when he hears the "hideous crash" of "senseless Ilium" falling as if in sympathy with Priam:

> For, lo! his sword,
> Which was declining on the milky head
> Of reverend Priam, seem'd i' th' air to stick.
> So, as a painted tyrant, Pyrrhus stood
> And, like a neutral to his will and matter,
> Did nothing.
> But, as we often see, against some storm,
> A silence in the heavens, the rack stand still,
> The bold winds speechless, and the orb below
> As hush as death, anon the dreadful thunder
> Doth rend the region; so, after Pyrrhus' pause,
> A roused vengeance sets him new a-work;

9. *The Question of Hamlet* (1959; reprinted New York, 1961), p. 157.

And never did the Cyclops' hammer fall
On Mars's armour, forg'd for proof eterne,
With less remorse than Pyrrhus' bleeding sword
Now falls on Priam.

[II.ii.471]

Hamlet, "like a neutral to his will and matter," has been hesitating in the acting of *his* revenge (for Pyrrhus, too, is a revenger); and Hamlet, too, has heard the "hideous crash" of a society's central edifice and symbol. The enacting of his revenge has come to seem like the cataclysm of an entire world.[10]

The momentary identification between Hamlet and Pyrrhus does not yet exhaust the image. Plays-within-a-play tend, I have suggested, to reflect the nature of dramatic art itself; they present an image, not only of this play's thematic concerns, but of this play as any or all plays. And thus the image of Pyrrhus as "painted tyrant"—an image associated, by the epithet, with forms of art—expresses something of the nature of the tragic drama. It is an image of energy in stasis, of an eternally suspended moment—suspended first because it is called "painted," and also because of the retarding motion of the verse here, with its long, swelling epic simile—an eternal moment preceding the inexorable fall of the tragic blow.

This static instant—which, while only an instant, is also an eternity fixed by poet and painter—is a demonstration of the esthetic fact that, in the Player's play, Troy will always fall, that Hecuba will always lament, and that the audience will always sympathize—and thus that Troy will never fall utterly. The permanence of the image, and of its potential effect upon an audience, is important in understanding Hamlet's reaction to it. Imaged in the pregnant instant of "Pyrrhus' pause" is the optimistic distinction between life and art expressed for our modern world by Pirandello: "All that lives, by the fact

10. On Pyrrhus as revenger, see Arthur Johnson, "The Player's Speech in *Hamlet*," *Shakespeare Quarterly* 13 (Winter 1962): 21–30: "Pyrrhus unites in his person the avenger of Paris' double crime of lust and murder of Pyrrhus' father, as Hamlet is the avenger of Claudius' double crime" (p. 24).

of living, has a form, and by the same token must die—except the work of art which lives forever in so far as it *is* form." [11]

In the world of flux and mere appearance which baffles Hamlet's search for an adequate expression, a play—apparently the most insubstantial of phenomena—moves Hamlet deeply. He wanted "a passionate speech," and that he surely got. Nor can we dismiss the Player's speech as mere literary travesty: whatever objections we might make to it—its strange words, overelaboration, emotional excess—are the same objections made by the audience at Elsinore, as if Shakespeare specifically wanted to forestall and disarm our criticism. Indeed the speech does (in Dryden's phrase) "smell too strongly of the buskin"; but, as Harry Levin recognizes,[12] this is an integral part of the *trompe l'oeil* effect by which the play-within-the-play makes the equally conventional primary play (that is, *Hamlet* itself) stand out as primary reality. The self-consciously "poetic" style of the Player's speech forces us to recognize it as something apart from Hamlet's accustomed world. Like Hamlet, savoring and questioning that word *mobled,* we are forced to attend to the language of the Player's speech: because it calls attention to itself as poetry, its language is "corporealized"; it pulls us up short as we confront those devices—its alliterations, invocations, epic similes, archaisms, and so on—which tell us that this is not the "transparent" language of ordinary discourse.[13] We need not like the language of the Player's speech, though I think we ought, but we cannot dismiss it. Hamlet, at least, does not.

Hamlet responds eagerly to this professional in the arts of expression. Indeed, he gives the Player the sincerest flattery: his imitation of the Player's speech follows after Polonius has been bid to "see the players well bestowed" and the stage is again clear. The similarity between Hamlet's soliloquy ("O, what a rogue and peasant slave am I!") and the Player's speech

11. Preface to *Six Characters in Search of an Author,* in *Naked Masks: Five Plays* ed. Eric Bentley (New York, 1952), p. 372.

12. *Question of Hamlet,* p. 161; Levin quotes Dryden.

13. I borrow the words *corporealized* and *transparent* from the chapter "The Poet as Fool and Priest," in Burkhardt's *Shakespearean Meanings.*

was noticed by Dover Wilson, who writes that "The two speeches are for all the world like a theme given out by the First Violin and then repeated by the soloist." [14] Repeated, however, with important variations. But the musical analogy is apt because the similarity between the player's speech and Hamlet's soliloquy is very much one of tone and rhythm.

Hamlet's speech, like the Player's, builds to a crescendo of sound and emotion:

> Am I a coward?
> Who calls me villain, breaks my pate across,
> Plucks off my beard and blows it in my face,
> Tweaks me by the nose, gives me the lie i' th' throat
> As deep as to the lungs? Who does me this?
> Ha!
> 'Swounds, I should take it; for it cannot be
> But I am pigeon-liver'd and lack gall
> To make oppression bitter, or ere this
> I should 'a fatted all the region kites
> With this slave's offal. Bloody, bawdy villain!
> Remorseless, treacherous, lecherous, kindless villain!
> O, vengeance!
>
> [II.ii.565]

And here Hamlet's speech, like the Player's at the instant when Pyrrhus's ear is taken prisoner, stops suddenly in its hurtling career. Hamlet, too, is caught in an attitude of listening, suspended while his own roaring declamation dies away. Then:

> Why, what an ass am I! This is most brave,
> That I, the son of a dear father murder'd,
> Prompted to my revenge by heaven and hell,
> Must, like a whore, unpack my heart with words,
> And fall a-cursing like a very drab,
> A scullion!
>
> [II.ii.578]

14. *What Happens in "Hamlet"* (New York, 1935), p. 214.

The moment of stasis ended, Hamlet's speech moves rapidly, surely, with a new sense of purpose, to the announcement of a plan of action. The conclusion comes as swiftly and irrevocably as Pyrrhus's deadly blow; and the speech which begins as a reflection on the nature of acting ends with the announcement of the tragic peripety: "The play's the thing / Wherein I'll catch the conscience of the King."

Something curious has happened between the two speeches: the variation on the theme. For the Player's speech, a speech that is decisively "play" and makes no illusory claims to be "real," is wholly successful in its expression; but, the "play" now over, the words of passion become in Hamlet's mouth a mere unpacking, a whorishness. And this, as Hamlet recognizes, is most strange. A player has moved himself and his audience to tears on behalf of a mere fiction; Hamlet now, at his most sincere and most truly impassioned, finds that his sincerity falls far short of a player's seeming, that his true passion is more theatrical and less satisfying than a player's part.

The question Hamlet puts initially stands halting between the existential and the purely esthetic:

> What's Hecuba to him or he to Hecuba,
> That he should weep for her? What would he do,
> Had he the motive and the cue for passion
> That I have?
>
> [II.ii.552]

And the quick answer he gives is as psychologically useless as it is esthetically naïve: "He would drown the stage with tears, / And cleave the general ear with horrid speech." Hamlet tries to do precisely this, as we have seen, going faster and faster, louder and louder, working himself up only to stop short and condemn himself for cursing "like a drab." What goes wrong? Why doesn't the Player's way work for Hamlet?

Since a part of Hamlet's perplexity has to do with the choice of words and their mode of delivery, a part of our answer must also deal with the linguistic medium. And so we may notice that the Player's old-fashioned declamation was alive in the timelessness of its play: it stood out from the general buzz and hum of Denmark's language and earned for itself the right to be attended to fully. But Hamlet is imprisoned in history, a fool of time, and his words are the realm's current coin. Hamlet's words are as good as such words can be, but (as he will later tell Laertes) anyone can "mouth" and "rant" them; and despite all the emphasis in the world, the loudest word in a worn-out language might as well be a whisper. At this stage of the action, we might say, Hamlet's play (unlike the Player's play of Pyrrhus and Priam) is not yet written: because he lives he is tied to a form, but it is the form of the dying animal; it is a form that lives in history, and so gives itself the lie at every successive moment of its being. Hamlet's passion becomes false in the very speaking of it, and this (we recall) is precisely the thing he feared when we first saw him, alone and silent, nursing that inner core of unexpressed truth which alone was trustworthy.

But there is more. For the expression Hamlet seeks is one that words alone could never accomplish. Hamlet demands an expression in action, and so we may notice that it is action which the Player's speech contains but Hamlet's lacks. Poet and painter have embodied the form of Pyrrhus's revenge, and when the Player speaks his lines, the words give renewed life to this action which has been made eternal form. But Hamlet has before him still the task of uniting the proper action with his words, of informing his words with meaning through gesture. Before the meeting with his father's ghost, Hamlet thought he must be content with what was within. Now the players have come and shown him the potential of "acting"; but immediately he has found the difficulty and double-edgedness of it. Not just any acting will do, and not all words. Still, somehow, "The play's the thing."

I am trying to find an answer to the question, "What does Hamlet find in the players' art?" and I am aware that the answer I am proposing is a tortuous one. I am aware, too, that

there is an easier answer: we could simply say that Hamlet
recalls a commonplace about the affective powers of drama—

> That guilty creatures, sitting at a play,
> Have by the very cunning of the scene
> Been struck so to the soul that presently
> They have proclaim'd their malefactions—
>   [II.ii.585]

and decides to use the theater as a sort of lie-detector test. Is
it, then, only a modern consciousness, seeing *Hamlet* through
the redactions of Pirandello or Tom Stoppard, which will
want to find more here than the obvious lesson in criminology?

The fact is that *Hamlet,* through any eyes, is insistently self-
conscious about its own histrionic basis. And in a theater like
Shakespeare's, where the metaphor of life-as-drama was never
far away, could the situation of Hamlet's soliloquy be dismissed?—a player in a play (the actor playing Hamlet in *Hamlet*) gives a speech about a player playing a player within his
play, and in that speech considers the relationships between
appearance and reality, histrionics and sincerity, acting and
action. A degree of subtlety seems warranted.

And there are other indications that the answer to Hamlet's questions about the players' art, his troubled "What
would he do, / Had he the motive and the cue for passion /
That I have?" involves more than simply proving Claudius's
guilt. For the lie-detector use of acting is one we see much
of in *Hamlet,* and though it shares certain characteristics with
Hamlet's use of acting, it is decisively not the same. Polonius
is the great master of it—of using, that is, the indirection or
downright falseness of acting to discover a truth. Polonius was
in his time an amateur actor himself; appropriately, he played
Caesar and was killed in the capitol. But we now see Polonius
either as a theater critic (and it is a flat sort of criticism he
practices, multiplying rigid categories while demanding that
he be kept entertained), or as a director—of Laertes, Reynaldo,
Ophelia, Gertrude. To each he recommends the use of seeming:
in the case of Laertes it is to be nothing short of a life-style, but
with the others it is specifically a means for getting at a

hidden truth. In itself, of course, there is nothing particularly wrong with his advise to use "indirections [to] find directions out." But the nature of the truth which is to be found out by these means is seriously inadequate. The truth is, for Polonius, a thing, a simple object, which the sufficiently deceptive man ought to be able to sneak up on and seize. "Give me up the truth," he demands of Ophelia (I.iii.98), and (underscoring the worth of a truth negotiable in this manner) he tells Reynaldo to use a "bait of falsehood [to] take this carp of truth" (II.i.62). He can boast:

> If circumstances lead me, I will find
> Where truth is hid, though it were hid indeed
> Within the centre.
>
> [II.ii.156]

The truth in this case is the truth of Hamlet's motives, and it is appropriate that the sort of discovery the Polonian roundaboutness is able to make is itself a circularity: "Mad call I it; for, to define true madness, / What is't but to be nothing else but mad?" (II.ii.93).

It is not, then, simply Polonius's habit of lurking behind arrases which is wrong. The mistake also comes in what he expects to find when he peeks from behind the arras onto the stage he has set. His belief in a unitary, capturable truth is in some ways similar to Hamlet's early belief in an inner core of essential being. But Polonius dies like a rat because he is too busy in his seeking to find anything; while Hamlet, both actor and observer of actors, learns a great lesson about ends and means: the hidden truth and the mode of discovery are one, Hamlet finds.

Polonius is not alone in his failings. Rosencrantz and Guildenstern also use dissembling to pluck out the heart of a mystery, and find that their acting only discovers an actor. Even those good soldiers on watch for the ghost in the opening scene were involved in the impossible search for answers to misstated questions. There is a lesson here for Hamlet, and one for us as well. When we approach the problem of Hamlet's delayed revenge—a problem more vexed than any ghost—

and try to pluck out the heart of that mystery, we would do
well to recall these epistemological muddles.

For are we not accustomed to thinking of Hamlet's task as
Polonius thinks of truth—as something simple and unitary,
capable of discovery although only, perhaps, after some initial
indirectness? In fact, as I have tried to show, the act of revenge is conceived, by Hamlet and his creator, as an expressive
act, a fully meaningful linguistic and gestural expression to be
undertaken in a world where words and gestures have become
largely meaningless. It is thus a creative as much as a destructive act, and is as complex and hard-won as all true acts of
creation must be. To consider the question of Hamlet's delayed revenge in a narrower context is to run the risk of feeling cheated by the play. Hamlet, after all, never does consciously overcome whatever scruples or fastidiousness have
kept him from his revenge; rather he stumbles into it when
the Claudius-Laertes plot misfires. Thus, a critic can write that
the duel, with all its attendant deaths, is mere "accident . . .
which breaks the chain of motivation." [15] But if not consciously willed, it is still no accident. Hamlet's protracted
search for "revenge" is the search, not for mere action however
bloody, but for fully expressive action. And what Hamlet finds
is that this action must be accomplished as the players accomplish theirs, with the facing and fulfilling of the tragedy's necessary fifth act.

In *Feeling and Form,* Susanne Langer defines "the tragic
rhythm" as "the pattern of a life that grows, flourishes, and declines." In tragedy, that universal life-rhythm "is abstracted by
being transferred . . . to the sphere of characteristically human action, where it is exemplified in mental and emotional
growth, maturation, and the final relinquishment of power."
And, Langer adds, "In that relinquishment lies the hero's true
'heroism'—the vision of life as accomplished, that is, life in
its entirety, the sense of fulfillment that lifts him above his

15. Brents Stirling, *Unity in Shakespearean Tragedy* (New York, 1956),
p. 72.

defeat." [16] To Hamlet, more perhaps than to any tragic hero except Oedipus, the search for the characteristic tragic rhythm becomes an almost self-conscious concern. Especially because of his interest in modes of playing, we are made to feel that Hamlet's quest (say, for revenge) is a quest for the shape of his own play, that Hamlet comes to recognize his subservience to the action, in the Aristotelian sense, for which he exists. Hamlet's task thus involves renunciation as well as action: that is the truth, both esthetic and existential, which he learns in part from his observation of the plays. "The readiness is all": in the tone of quiet acceptance which characterizes Hamlet in the play's closing moments we see the fruits of that observation. [17]

An aspect of Hamlet's task has been to join the language of words to the proper language of gesture. And no gesture short of the final tragic gesture, Hamlet's death, will suffice. It is not only Claudius who must expiate the murder of old Hamlet, but Hamlet who must succeed a Hamlet as tragic victim. As the overdetermined image of Pyrrhus in the Player's speech suggests, avenger and victim must finally become one. Hamlet dies, and his death, the necessary end of his tragedy, enables his expressive gesture. Now to the living, to that steadfast and scholarly observer Horatio, falls the burden to report Hamlet and his cause aright. But then, Horatio's task has really been accomplished already, for (as Northrop Frye writes), "At the end of *Hamlet* we get a strong feeling that the play we are watching is, in a sense, Horatio's story." [18] Hamlet achieves his necessary language with the completion, in death, when the time is ripe, of his tragic play. That language becomes ours, as it does Horatio's, to be delivered by us "aright / To the unsatisfied" (V.ii.331).

16. *Feeling and Form* (New York, 1953), p. 356.

17. On the changed mood in the play's closing moments, see Maynard Mack's influential article "The World of Hamlet," *Yale Review* 41 (Summer 1952): 502–23. And cf. Fergusson, *Idea of a Theater*, p. 144: "One could say that [Hamlet] feels the poetic rightness of his own death."

18. *Fools of Time* (Toronto, 1967), p. 31.

3

Julius Caesar

In the previous chapter I suggested that the answer to the problems Hamlet confronts is *Hamlet* itself: the perfected form of the play successfully subsumes, and in that sense solves, the various linguistic crises within it. Now having with one hand put forward this purely formal, esthetic answer, I want with the other hand to begin, tentatively, to withdraw it. I would like, that is, to have the position reached in the discussion of *Hamlet* to be maintained provisionally as a possibility: it has, I believe, its portion of truth, but it is no shame to confess that, as with most things Shakespearean, it must share its truth with other, competing truths. The limited nature of this particular truth is indicated by my own characterization of it as formal and esthetic; for the question which immediately occurs is whether any such "truth" (the only standard for which remains that offered by Keats's Grecian Urn) can be wholly satisfying.

In regard to theories of tragedy, Murray Krieger asks "whether we have not been beguiled by aesthetic satisfactions and whether the utterly stripped tragic vision may not after all be less illusory than the fullness which shines through tragedy." [1] He suggests, that is, that tragedy's "calm of mind, all passion spent" is the result of a formal resolution which may be at odds with the play's "stripped" thematic content. Similarly, Clifford Leech remarks that "the control of art need suggest nothing more than that man has a certain faculty for ordering his experience: it does not transform the nature of that experience, and it does not necessarily suggest that either he

1. *The Tragic Vision* (New York, 1960), p. 21.

or a creator can control the totality of experience." [2] Now I am not convinced that the stripping of an artist's vision is a worthwhile pursuit, nor do I underestimate the importance of our ability to order even parts of our experience; still, the objections which have been leveled against a formalist approach to tragedy are powerful and cannot be dismissed.

In the next chapter, on *Troilus and Cressida,* I intend to give these objections their due: in that play, I will argue, Shakespeare himself is most fully skeptical about the possibility of substituting the control of art for the chaos of experience. But even with *Hamlet* I must acknowledge the presence of this alternative. Conceived in formal terms, the ending of *Hamlet* ought, indeed, to leave us satisfied, filled with the sense that, yes, we have come through—that, yes, the world is once again in joint. Yet even as the trumpets sound and Hamlet is borne like a soldier to the stage, certain doubts may refuse to be stilled. How appropriate, really, is this military fanfare for the Hamlet we have known? Can the brash Fortinbras ever be expected to understand the story which the scholarly Horatio is bid to tell? Though our passion is spent in the tragic close, is there not also the hint of mere waste? Fortinbras, we may even suspect, is more appropriately the heir to Claudius's limitations than to Hamlet's brilliance. At the same instant that Shakespeare affirms the order which his play has brought out of chaos, he subtly mocks the pretension of that affirmation.

In *Julius Caesar,* to which we now turn, a similar doubleness emerges. But the critic, who is fated to the discursive mode, cannot speak (Weird Sister-like) simultaneously of two opposite truths. I have chosen, therefore, to follow out the basic pattern we have seen in *Hamlet.* I will speak as if a formal, esthetic solution were indeed possible for the various linguistic problems we discover, and locate that solution in the fullness of the tragic form. At the end of the discussion, before proceeding to *Troilus and Cressida,* I will recur to the

2. *Shakespeare's Tragedies and Other Studies in Seventeenth Century Drama* (London, 1950), p. 8.

other possibility, Shakespeare's recognition of the insufficiency of the formal solution. In *Troilus and Cressida* that latter recognition is primary in Shakespeare's treatment of his material; in *Hamlet* and *Julius Caesar* it remains a muted, troubling doubt.

In *Julius Caesar* we find, more starkly and simply than in *Hamlet,* those problems of communication and expression, those confusions linguistic and ritualistic, which mark the world of the tragedies. The play opens with the sort of apparently expository scene in which Shakespeare actually gives us the major action of the play in miniature. Flavius and Marullus, the tribunes, can barely understand the punning language of the commoners; had they the wit, they might exclaim with Hamlet, "Equivocation will undo us." It is ostensibly broad daylight in Rome, but the situation is dreamlike; for although the language which the two classes speak is phonetically identical, it is, semantically, two separate languages. The cobbler's language, though it sounds like the tribunes', is (to the tribunes) a sort of inexplicable dumb show.

And as with words, so with gestures; the certainties of ceremonial order are as lacking in Rome, as are the certainties of the verbal language. The commoners present an anomaly to the tribunes simply by walking "Upon a labouring day without the sign / Of [their] profession." To the commoners it is a "holiday," to the tribunes (although in fact it is the Feast of Lupercal), a "labouring day." The commoners have planned an observance of Caesar's triumph—itself, to the tribunes, no triumph but rather a perversion of Roman order—but the tribunes send the "idle creatures" off to perform a quite different ceremony:

> Go, go, good countrymen, and for this fault
> Assemble all the poor men of our sort;
> Draw them to Tiber banks, and weep your tears
> Into the channel, till the lowest stream
> Do kiss the most exalted shores of all.
>
> [I.i.57]

Thus, in a Rome where each man's language is foreign to the next, ritual gestures are converted into their opposites; confusion in the state's symbolic system makes every action perilously ambiguous. The tribunes, having turned the commoners' planned ritual into its opposite, go off bravely to make their own gesture, to "Disrobe the images" of Caesar; but shortly we learn that they have actually been made to play parts in a bloodier ritual (one which, as we shall see, becomes increasingly common in the play). And when, in a later scene, we find Brutus deciding upon *his* proper gesture, the confusions of this first scene should recur to us.[3]

The second scene again opens with mention of specifically ritual observance, as Caesar bids Calphurnia stand in Antony's way to receive the touch which will "Shake off [her] sterile curse" (I.ii.9). Perhaps Shakespeare intends to satirize Caesar's superstitiousness; at least we can say that Calphurnia's sterility and the fructifying touch introduce the question, what sort of ritual can assure (political) succession in Rome? Directly, the Soothsayer steps forth, warning Caesar, "Beware the ides of March." But this communication is not understood: "He is a dreamer; Let us leave him. Pass" (I.ii.24).

What follows, when Caesar and his train have passed off the stage leaving Brutus and Cassius behind, is an enactment —virtually an iconic presentation—of the linguistic problem. More clearly even than the first scene, this scene gives us the picture of Rome as a place where words and rituals have dangerously lost their conventional meanings. As Cassius begins to feel out Brutus about the conspiracy—telling him of Rome's danger and wishes, of Caesar's pitiful mortality, of Brutus's republican heritage—their conversation is punctuated by shouts from offstage, shouts at whose meaning they can only guess. (The situation brings to mind the one in *Hamlet* when the men on the battlements question each other about the strange new customs in Denmark.)

3. Cf. the discussion of this scene, and of "mock-ceremony" generally in the play, in Brents Stirling, *Unity in Shakespearean Tragedy* (New York, 1956).

Casca, an eyewitness to the ritual in the marketplace, finally arrives to be their interpreter; but even he has understood imperfectly. Caesar (he says) has been offered the crown, but

> I can as well be hang'd as tell the manner of it: it was mere foolery; I did not mark it. I saw Mark Antony offer him a crown—yet 'twas not a crown neither, 'twas one of these coronets. . . .   [I.ii.234]

Caesar refused the crown, but Casca suspects "he would fain have had it." "The rabblement hooted," and Caesar "swooned and fell down at" the stench. As for the rest, Cicero spoke, but again the language problem intervened: "He spoke Greek." There is other news: "Marullus and Flavius, for pulling scarfs off Caesar's images, are put to silence." And, "There was more foolery yet, if I could remember it" (I.ii.286).

The dramatic point of it all lies not so much in the conflict between republican and monarchical principles, as in the sheer confusion of the reported and overheard scene. It is all hooting and clapping and uttering of bad breath, swooning, foaming at the mouth, and speaking Greek. Casca's cynical tone is well suited to the occasion, for the farcical charade of the crown-ritual, with Caesar's refusal and Antony's urging, is itself a cynical manipulation. The crowd clapped and hissed "as they use to do the players in the theatre" (I.ii.260)—and rightly so.

These two opening scenes give us the world in which Brutus is to undertake his great gesture. When we next see Brutus, his decision is made: "It must be by his death" (II.i.10). Behind Brutus's decision is that linguistic and ceremonial confusion which is comic in the case of the commoners and sinister in the case of Caesar's crown-ritual. The innovations in Rome's ceremonial order give evidence to Brutus for the necessity of his gesture. But those same innovations, attesting to a failure in Rome's basic linguistic situation, also make it most probable that his gesture will fail. Brutus is not unlike Hamlet: he is a man called upon to make an expressive gesture in a world where the commensurate values necessary to expression are lacking. The killing of Caesar, despite the honorable intentions that are within Brutus and passing show, will thus be only one more ambiguous, misunderstood action in a world where no action can have an assured value. Brutus's grand expression might as well be Greek in this Roman world.

Brutus's position is not unlike Hamlet's, but he does not see what Hamlet sees. Indeed, he does not even see as much as his fellow conspirators do. To Cassius, the dreadful and unnatural storm over Rome reflects "the work we have in hand" (I.iii.129); to the thoughtful Cassius, the confusion in the heavens is an aspect of the confusion in Rome. But Brutus is, typically, unmoved by the storm, and calmly makes use of its strange light to view the situation: "The exhalations, whizzing in the air, / Give so much light that I may read by them" (II.i.44). And what he reads by this deceptive light is as ambiguous as the shouts of the crowd at the crown-ritual: the paper bears temptations slipped into his study by the conspirators, words that mislead and may betray. On the basis of this mysterious communication, revealed by a taper's dim light and the unnatural "exhalations" above, Brutus determines to "speak and strike." Every sign is misinterpreted by Brutus; and the world that seems to him to make a clear demand for words and gestures is in fact a world where words are equivocal and where gestures quickly wither into their opposites.

The situation, as I have so far described it, forces upon us the question critics of the play have most frequently debated: who is the play's hero? A simple enough question, it would seem: the title tells us that this is *The Tragedy of Julius Caesar*. But that answer only serves to show the actual complexity of the question, for if Caesar (who is, after all, dead by the middle of the play) is to this play what, say, Hamlet is to his, then *Julius Caesar* is, structurally at least, a most peculiar tragedy. The question of the hero—and a glance at the critical literature shows that the position is indeed questionable—bears upon fundamental matters of meaning and structure.[4]

Now it is a curious fact about Shakespeare's plays (and, to an extent, about all drama) that the questions the critics ask have a way of duplicating the questions the characters ask, as though the playwright had done his best to make all criticism redundant. As if the play were not enough, nor the characters sufficient unto their conflicts, the critical audience continues to fight the same fights and ask the same questions the characters in the play do. Of *Julius Caesar*, as I have said, the question we most often ask concerns the play's hero: Caesar or Brutus? I have not bothered to tally the choices; for our purposes it is more interesting to notice the mode of critical procedure and the way in which it tends to imitate the actions of the characters in the play. Both critics and characters tend to choose sides in their respective conflicts on the bases of political prejudice and evaluations of moral rectitude. Since the moral and political issues in *Julius Caesar* are themselves eternally moot, it is not surprising that the critical debate continues unresolved.

About Caesar, for instance: if we try to make our determination of herohood on the basis of Caesar's moral stature, we are doing precisely what the characters do; and we find, I think,

4. Herewith a brief sampler of alternatives. John Dover Wilson, in his New Cambridge edition of the play (Cambridge, 1949) finds that "the play's theme is the single one, Liberty *versus* Tyranny." Since Dover Wilson believes that "Caesarism is a secular threat to the human spirit," it obviously follows that Brutus is our hero (pp. xxi–xxii). But the editor of the Arden *Julius Caesar,* T. S. Dorsch (London, 1955), while admitting that "Caesar has some weaknesses," thinks that the assassination is an "almost incredible piece of criminal folly," for (he asks confidently), "Can it be doubted that Shakespeare wishes us to admire his Caesar?" (p. xxxviii–xxxix). Another approach is tried by R. A. Foakes: "The three main characters are all noble and yet weak; none has the stature of hero or villian" ("An Approach to *Julius Caesar,*" *Shakespeare Quarterly* 5 [Summer 1954]: 270). And, for the sake of symmetry, a final example: "There are . . . two tragic heroes in *Julius Caesar,* Brutus and Caesar, although one is more fully treated than the other" (Irving Ribner, *Patterns in Shakespearian Tragedy* [London, 1960], p. 56).

that he becomes for us what he is for Shakespeare's Romans, less a man than the object of men's speculations. Caesar is the Colossus whose legs we may peep about but whom we can never know; characters and audience alike peep assiduously, each giving us a partial view which simply will not accord with any other. Within the play, Caesar is virtually constituted of the guesses made about him: Casca's rude mockery, Cassius's sneers, Brutus's composite portrait of the present Caesar (against whom he knows no wrong) and the dangerous serpent of the future, Antony's passionate defense, the mob's fickle love and hate: these are the guesses, and contradictory as they are, they give us the Caesar of the play—and of the play's critics.

Of Caesar's, or for that matter of Brutus's, moral status we can have little more certain knowledge than the characters themselves have. What we are in a privileged position to know is the *structure* of the play: the characters' prison, the play's encompassing form, is our revelation. What I propose to do, therefore, is to look at the implicit answer Brutus gives (through his actions) to the question, who is the play's tragic hero?, and compare that answer to the answer revealed by the play's unfolding structure.

Everything Brutus does (until the collapse of the conspiracy) is calculated to justify the title of the play, to make it indeed *The Tragedy of Julius Caesar*. As we watch Brutus directing the conspiracy, we watch a man plotting a typical Shakespearean tragedy; and it is crucial to the success of his plot that Caesar indeed be its hero-victim. The assassination, as Brutus conceives it, must have all the solemnity and finality of a tragic play. The wonder of the spectacle must, as in tragedy, join the audience (both within and without the play) into a community of assent to the deed. For his part, Brutus is content with a necessary secondary role, the mere agent of the hero's downfall—a kind of Laertes, or a more virtuous Aufidius to Caesar's Coriolanus.

But of course Brutus's plot (in both senses of the word) is a failure. The withholding of assent by the audience (again,

both within and without the play) proves his failure more con-
clusively than do moral or political considerations. Brutus
misunderstands the language of Rome; he misinterprets all the
signs both cosmic and earthly; and the furthest reach of his
failure is his failure to grasp, until the very end, the destined
shape of his play. Brutus's plot is a failure, but by attending
to the direction he tries to give it we can find, ironically, a
clear anatomy of the typical tragic action.

Brutus makes his decision and in Act II, scene 1 he meets
with the conspirators. Decius puts the question, "Shall no man
else be touch'd but only Caesar?". Cassius, whose concerns are
wholly practical, urges Antony's death. But Brutus demurs:
the assassination as he conceives it has a symbolic dimension as
important as its practical dimension; and although Brutus is
not able to keep the two clearly separated (he opposes Antony's death partly out of concern for the deed's appearance
"to the common eyes") he is clear about the need for a single
sacrificial victim. His emphasis on sacrifice indicates the ritual
shape Brutus hopes to give the assassination:

> Let's be sacrificers, but not butchers, Caius.
> We all stand up against the spirit of Caesar,
> And in the spirit of men there is no blood.
> O that we then could come by Caesar's spirit,
> And not dismember Caesar! But, alas,
> Caesar must bleed for it! And, gentle friends,
> Let's kill him boldly, but not wrathfully;
> Let's carve him as a dish fit for the gods,
> Not hew him as a carcass fit for hounds. . . .
> We shall be call'd purgers, but not murderers.
>
> [II.i.166, 180]

The "sacrifice" must not be confused with murder, with mere
butchery. The name of the deed becomes all important, in-
dicating the distance betwen a gratuitous, essentially meaningless gesture, and a sanctioned, efficacious, unambiguous ritual.

But Brutus's speech, with a fine irony, betrays his own fatal
confusion. "In the spirit of men there is no blood," but in this

spirit—this symbol, this embodiment of Caesarism—there is, "alas," as much blood as Lady Macbeth will find in Duncan. Whatever we may feel about Brutus's political intentions, we must acknowledge a failure which has, it seems to me, as much to do with logic and language as with politics: Brutus is simply unclear about the difference between symbols and men. And his confusion, which leads to the semantic confusion between "murder" and "sacrifice," and between meaningless gestures and sanctioned ritual, is the central case of something we see at every social level in Rome. The assassination Brutus plans as a means of purging Rome dwindles to just more of the old ambiguous words and empty gestures. The assassination loses its intended meaning as surely as the commoners' celebration did in scene 1.

The assassination is surrounded by Brutus with all the rhetoric and actions of a sacrificial rite. It becomes ritually and literally a bloodbath, as Brutus bids,

> Stoop, Romans, stoop,
> And let us bathe our hands in Caesar's blood
> Up to the elbows, and besmear our swords.
> [III.i.106]

Even the disastrous decision to allow Antony to address the mob arises from Brutus's concern that "Caesar shall / Have all true rites and lawful ceremonies" (III.i.241). In Brutus's plot, where Caesar is the hero-victim whose death brings tragedy's "calm of mind, all passion spent," no one, not even Antony, should be left out of the ceremonious finale. With the conspirators' ritualized bloodbath, indeed, the implied metaphor of the assassination-as-drama becomes explicit—if also horribly ironic:

> *Cas.* Stoop then, and wash. How many ages hence
> Shall this our lofty scene be acted over
> In states unborn and accents yet unknown!
> *Bru.* How many times shall Caesar bleed in sport. . . .
> [III.i.112]

Trapped in their bloody pageant, these histrionic conspirators
cannot see what, in the terms they themselves suggest, is the
most important point of all: this lofty scene occurs, not at the
end, but in the middle of a tragic play.

Brutus's plot is not Shakespeare's; and immediately after
the conspirators have acted out what should be the denoue-
ment of their tragic play, the actual shape of the play (the one
they cannot see as such) begins to make itself clear. Antony,
pointedly recalling Brutus's distinction between "sacrificers"
and "butchers," says to the slaughtered symbol of tyranny, "O,
pardon me, thou bleeding piece of earth, / That I am meek
and gentle with these butchers!" (III.i.255), and announces the
further course of the action:

> And Caesar's spirit, ranging for revenge,
> With Ate by his side come hot from hell,
> Shall in these confines with a monarch's voice
> Cry 'Havoc!' and let slip the dogs of war,
> That this foul deed shall smell above the earth
> With carrion men, groaning for burial.
>
> [III.i.271]

Brutus's revolutionary gesture, which was intended to bring to
birth a stabler order, has been (in an esthetic as well as a political sense) premature. His ritual has failed, and now, as
Caesar's spirit ranges for revenge (for there *is* blood in the
spirits of men), it still remains for the proper ritual to be
found. Now Brutus will at last assume his proper role: Brutus
must be our tragic hero.

Of course he does his best to deny that role. His stoicism—
the coolness, for instance, with which he dismisses Caesar's
ghost: "Why, I will see thee at Philippi, then" (IV.iii.284)—is
hardly what we expect of the grandly suffering tragic hero.
Still, it is to Brutus that we owe one of the finest descriptions
of the peculiar moment in time occupied by a Shakespearean
tragedy:

> Since Cassius first did whet me against Caesar,
> I have not slept.

> Between the acting of a dreadful thing
> And the first motion, all the interim is
> Like a phantasma or a hideous dream.
> The Genius and the mortal instruments
> Are then in council; and the state of man,
> Like to a little kingdom, suffers then
> The nature of an insurrection.
>
> [II.i.61]

The moment is suspended, irresolute, but charged with the energy to complete itself. The separation of "acting" from "first motion," of "Genius" from "mortal instruments," is an intolerable state—the measure of it is the insomnia—which demands resolution. In *Macbeth* we will see this moment protracted and anatomized; it is the tragic moment, and Brutus, for all his Roman calm, must pass through it to its necessary completion.

The acting of the "dreadful thing"—or, rather, what Brutus thinks is the dreadful thing, Caesar's death—does not bring the promised end; that is made immediately clear. Antony's funeral oration shows that Brutus's grand gesture has changed little. Antony easily converts Brutus's sacrifice into murder. In Rome (as in Elsinore) men's actions merely "seem," and Antony can shift the intended meaning of Brutus's action as easily as the tribunes had changed the intended meaning of the commoner's actions in Act I, scene 1. Antony can use virtually the same words as the conspirators—he can still call Brutus an "honourable man" and Caesar "ambitious"—and yet make condemnation of approval and approval of condemnation. Even after the revolutionary moment of Caesar's death, this Rome is all of a piece: a volatile mob, empty ceremonies, and a language as problematic as the reality it describes.

Even names are problematic here. It was with names that Cassius first went to work on Brutus:

> 'Brutus' and 'Caesar'. What should be in that 'Caesar'?
> Why should that name be sounded more than yours?
> Write them together: yours is as fair a name.

Sound them: it doth become the mouth as well.
Weigh them: it is as heavy. Conjure with 'em:
'Brutus' will start a spirit as soon as 'Caesar'.

[I.ii.142]

Cassius's contemptuous nominalism reminds one of Edmund
in *King Lear,* who also thinks that one name—that of "bastard," for instance—is as good as any other. Names, to Cassius
and Edmund, are conventional signs having reference to no
absolute value, and they may be manipulated at will.

In his funeral oration, Antony also plays freely with names;
and with the repetition of those two names "Brutus" and
"Caesar" he does indeed conjure a spirit. It is the spirit of
riot, of random violence, and its first victim (with a grotesque
appropriateness) is a poet and a name:

3 Pleb.   Your name sir, truly.
Cin.   Truly, my name is Cinna.
1 Pleb.   Tear him to pieces; he's a conspirator!
Cin.   I am Cinna the poet, I am Cinna the poet.
4 Pleb.   Tear him for his bad verses, tear him for his bad
verses!
Cin.   I am not Cinna the conspirator.
4 Pleb.   It is no matter, his name's Cinna; pluck but
his name out of his heart, and turn him going.
3 Pleb.   Tear him, tear him!

[III.iii.26]

"Pluck but his name out of his heart, and turn him going": it
is like Brutus's impossible, "And in the spirit of men there is
no blood." Again, it is the confusion between symbol and
reality, between the abstract name and the blood-filled man
who bears it. Poets, whose genius it is to mediate symbol and
reality and to find the appropriate name to match all things,
generally have rough going in *Julius Caesar*. Brutus the lib-
erator shows how he has insensibly aged into a figure indistin-
guishable from the tyrant when he dismisses a peace-making
poet with a curt, "What should the wars do with these jigging

fools?" (IV.iii.135). And Caesar, too, had rebuffed a poetical
soothsayer.

The gratuitous murder of Cinna the poet reflects ironically
upon the murder of Caesar. The poet's rending at the hands
of the mob is unreasonable, based solely on a confusion of
identities (of names, words), and while it bears some resem-
blance to the sacrifice of a scapegoat figure, it is really no
sacrifice at all but unsanctioned murder. Caesar's death, similarly, was undertaken as a sacrificial gesture, but quickly became identified with plain butchery. In the mirror of the
Cinna episode the assassination is seen as only one case in a
series of perverted rituals—a series that runs with increasing
frequency now, until the proper victim and the proper form
are at last found.

Immediately following the murder of Cinna we see the new
triumvirate pricking the names of its victims. The death of
Caesar has released the motive force behind the tragedy, and
that force runs unchecked now until the final sacrifice at
Philippi. From the very first scene of the play we have witnessed ritual gestures that wither into meaninglessness; with
the conspiracy and Caesar's death, we become aware of
sacrifice as the particular ritual toward which the world of the
play is struggling: the series of mistaken rituals becomes a
series of mistaken sacrifices, culminating at Philippi.[5]

The wrong sacrifice, the wrong victim: the play offers an
astonishing gallery of them. It has been noticed that all of the
major characters implicate themselves in this central action:

5. John Holloway does not discuss *Julius Caesar* in his *The Story of the
Night* (Lincoln, Neb., 1961), but his description of the sacrificial pattern
of Shakespearean tragedy is pertinent. That pattern "has as its centre a
very distinctive role pursued by the protagonist over the whole course of
the play: a role which takes him from being the cynosure of his society
to being estranged from it, and takes him, through a process of increasing alienation, to a point at which what happens to him suggests the
expulsion of a scapegoat, or the sacrifice of a victim, or something of
both" (p. 135). The audience can see that this pattern (which Brutus
tries to impose on *his* "Tragedy of Julius Caesar") more aptly describes
Brutus's career than Caesar's.

each character in the political quartet in turn makes a
similar kind of theatrical gesture implying the sacrifice of
his own life: to top his refusal of the crown, Caesar offers
the Roman mob his throat to cut; Brutus shows the same
people that he has a dagger ready for himself, in case
Rome should need his death; with half-hidden irony, Antony begs his death of the conspirators; and in the quarrel
scene, Cassius gives his "naked breast" for Brutus to
strike.[6]

The idea of sacrifice is imagistically linked to the idea of
hunters and the hunted. Caesar, says Antony, lies "like a deer
strucken by many princes" (III.i.210). The ruthless Octavius
feels, improbably enough, that he is "at the stake, / And bay'd
about with many enemies" (IV.i.48). But it was the conspirators themselves who first suggested the analogy between sacrifice and hunting: their blood-bathing ceremony suggests (as
Antony makes explicit) the actions of a hunter with his first
kill. And finally, appropriately, the sacrifice-hunting imagery
fastens on Brutus: "Our enemies have beat us to the pit"
(V.v.23).

From a slightly different perspective, the final scenes at
Philippi might be a comedy of errors. Military bungles and
mistaken identities follow quickly on each other's heels; the
number of suicides, especially, seems excessive. Of the suicide
of Titinius, a relatively minor character, Granville-Barker
asks, "why, with two suicides to provide for, Shakespeare
burdened himself with this third?"[7] The answer to his question, and the explanation for the apparent excesses generally,
must be found, I believe, in the context of false sacrifice
throughout the play. Caesar's death was one such false sacrifice; Cinna the poet's a horrible mistake; the political murders by the triumvirate continued the chain; and now Cassius
sacrifices himself on the basis of a mistake, while Titinius

6. Adrien Bonjour, *The Structure of "Julius Caesar"* (Liverpool, 1958),
p. 30, n. 33.

7. *Prefaces to Shakespeare* (Princeton, N.J., 1947), 2 : 401.

follows out of loyalty to the dead Cassius. Brutus embarked on the conspiracy because he misinterpreted the confused signs in, and above, Rome; the intended meaning of his own gesture was in turn subverted by Antony and the mob. And now Cassius has misinterpreted the signs: friendly troops are mistaken for hostile, their shouts of joy are not understood; thus "Caesar, thou art reveng'd," as Cassius dies, in error, "Even with the sword that kill'd thee" (V.iii.45). And, because Cassius has "misconstrued every thing" (as Titinius puts it [V.iii.84]), Titinius now dies, bidding, "Brutus, come apace."

Titinius places a garland on the dead Cassius before he dies himself; and Brutus, entering when both are dead, pronounces a solemn epitaph:

> Are yet two Romans living such as these?
> The last of all the Romans, fare thee well!
> It is impossible that ever Rome
> Should breed thy fellow. Friends, I owe moe tears
> To this dead man than you shall see me pay.
> I shall find time, Cassius, I shall find time.
> [V.iii.98]

The words and the actions form an appropriate tragic device of wonder—but this is no more the end than it was when Brutus spoke an epitaph for Caesar. The death of Cassius is still not the proper sacrifice, and the play has still to reach its culminating ritual.

At Philippi, Brutus at last accepts his role. Against the wishes of Cassius, Brutus insists upon meeting the enemy even before (as the enemy puts it), "we do demand of them." The ghost of Caesar has appeared and Brutus has accepted its portent: "I know my hour is come" (V.v.20). Most significant in Brutus's final speeches is their tone of acceptance:

> Countrymen,
> My heart doth joy that yet in all my life
> I found no man but he was true to me.
> I shall have glory by this losing day,

More than Octavius and Mark Antony
By this vile conquest shall attain unto.
So fare you well at once; for Brutus' tongue
Hath almost ended his life's history.
Night hangs upon mine eyes; my bones would rest,
That have but labour'd to attain this hour.

[V.v.33]

The expressed idea of the glorious defeat is an authentic sign
of Shakespearean tragedy: in a later play, Cleopatra will address similar lines to the wretchedly victorious Octavius. Brutus recognizes here the necessary end of "his life's history": all,
from the very start, has tended to this gesture. In it we may
find, as in Hamlet's death, "the vision of life in its entirety,
the sense of fulfillment that lifts [the hero] above his defeat." [8]
Brutus's death is the action which resolves the phantasmal
"interim" and ends the "insurrection" in "the state of man."

And this gesture receives, as the assassination of Caesar did
not, the requisite assent. Brutus "hath honour by his death,"
says Strato; and Lucilius, "So Brutus should be found." The
opposing parties join together now in Octavius's service, and
it is Antony himself who can pronounce the epitaph, "This
was the noblest Roman of them all." His words and the gestures are universally accepted.

But what of Rome and its future? I said at the outset of
this chapter that the esthetic satisfaction of the perfected
tragic form is a "truth" to be accepted only provisionally—
and it is the close involvement of Julius Caesar with widely
known historical facts which forces upon us the recognition of
that truth's limitations. Indeed, the play contains hints—
the bloody, divisive course of the triumvirate has been made
plain, for instance—which, even without prior historical
knowledge, might make us temper our optimism over the
play's conclusion. With Brutus's death the play has revealed its
tragic entelechy; the destined shape has been found, and the

8. Langer, *Feeling and Form* (New York, 1953), p. 356.

discovery brings its esthetic satisfactions. That the price of our pleasure is the hero's death is not (as in *King Lear* it will so terribly be) a source of discomfort. But what we cannot dismiss is our knowledge that every end is also a beginning. History will have its way; "fate" will defeat men's "wills"; and the "glory" of this "losing day" will tarnish and become, in the movement of time, as ambiguous as the glorious loss on the ides of March.

Thus we must entertain two apparently opposite points of view. With Brutus's sacrificial gesture the ritual has been found which can satisfy the dramatic expectations created by the play. The final words are spoken, the language is understood; and thus the play has given us what Robert Frost demanded of all poetry, "a momentary stay against confusion." But if we stress in Frost's definition his modifying word *momentary*, we find ourselves cast back upon history; and once out of the timeless world of the play, "confusion" predominates. Shakespeare, I believe, recognized this. In *Hamlet* we saw some aspects of his meditation on the problem of time. In *Troilus and Cressida* we will see more, and see in particular some ramifications of that problem for the nature of his art.

4

Troilus and Cressida

The exception that proves a rule is always a valuable find, and *Troilus and Cressida* (which seems an exception to so many rules) is therefore valuable to a study of Shakespearean tragedy. Shakespeare makes his characters' problems of expression more acute here than in almost any other of his plays. Words—often very difficult, "knotty" words, and an overwhelming profusion of them—are expended by the characters in a fruitless attempt to make sense of a senseless situation. On both sides, Trojan and Greek, the effort to rationalize, to understand, to manage events with words, goes on almost unceasingly, while events—the quite irrational actions of the play—take their own way with little regard to what is spoken.

In this world, rituals become mere games, with rules that can be adjusted at will. The war itself is a tedious and pointless business, and is felt to be so by men on both sides; it threatens to go on endlessly and resolve nothing. The play's great central ceremony—the battle between the champions Hector and Achilles—dwindles into a "sportful combat" between the wrong opponents, leaving the spectators with "expectance . . . what further [they] will do." The only decisive actions of the play occur specifically as violations of order, perversions of ceremony's formal expressiveness: both Cressida's treachery and Hector's death at the hands of Achilles's Myrmidons seem gratuitous and inexplicable. Language and gesture, which are from the beginning inadequate to the characters' needs, grow increasingly so and are never reformed. A world is fragmented in *Troilus and Cressida* and never reunited, leaving the audience, too, with expectance of what might follow. The conditions for tragedy are present in abundance, but the fulfilling resolution of tragedy is withheld.

The play is, then, a "problem": the designation is hard to avoid. From the start, its genre has been problematic. The Quarto of 1609 titles it a history; the Folio (1623), a tragedy; while the "Never Writer" who addresses himself to the "Ever Reader" with "News" in the dedicatory epistle (Q) calls it a witty play worthy of comparison with "the best comedy in Terence or Plautus."

When we turn to the play itself, this same confusion as to the nature of the beast confronts us almost immediately. The Prologue—armed for war "In like conditions as our argument" (25)—promises

> that our play
> Leaps o'er the vaunt and firstlings of those broils,
> Beginning in the middle; starting thence away
> To what may be digested in a play.
>
> [26]

Our expectations are thus raised for a scene of battle and high daring, a confrontation between "The princes orgillous, their high blood chaf'd," and the "sons of Troy"; but our first leap into the play proper only lands us in trouble. For instead of a warrior speaking in the terms and tones of war, we find a young man declaiming in the tones of romantic self-indulgence. Troilus's occupation is gone; he is not for the wars but for love:

> Call here my varlet; I'll unarm again.
> Why should I war without the walls of Troy
> That find such cruel battle here within?
> Each Troyan that is master of his heart,
> Let him to field; Troilus, alas, hath none.
>
> [I.i.1]

The Prologue, whose speech and bearing and costume are all (as he points out) fitted to the theme of war, has implicitly introduced the notion of poetic decorum—but how lacking in

decorum, for this occasion, is Troilus's elaborately rhetorical
courtly lover's speech!

> The Greeks are strong, and skilful to their strength,
> Fierce to their skill, and to their fierceness valiant;
> But I am weaker than a woman's tear,
> Tamer than sleep, fonder than ignorance,
> Less valiant than the virgin in the night,
> And skilless as unpractis'd infancy.
>
> [I.i.7]

The Prologue speaks the language of war, and the language
appropriate to a play about war; Troilus speaks the language of
a special sort of love; and now, to shatter further the decorum
of a play that has already begun indecorously enough, we hear
the voice of Pandarus, speaking its quite vulgar prose. To
Pandarus, the course of Troilus's wooing is like the preparation of something no more extraordinary than a cake, and the
lover "must needs tarry the grinding," the bolting, the leaven-
ing, the kneading, "the heating of the oven, and the baking,"
and even the cooling, "or you many chance to burn your lips"
(I.i.16–26). The contrast between Troilus's verse and Pandarus's prose is striking, and both stand in contrast to the expectations raised by the Prologue. Thus with its very first lines,
the play suggests that the lack of an adequate, appropriate
language will be—purposely, I believe—a part of its "problem."

And it is a problem outside the walls of Troy as well as
within. Scene 3 introduces us to the Greeks, met in council
to consider their deteriorating position in the war. Agamemnon
speaks first; he wants to hearten his troops with the thought
that the best-laid plans of men and Greeks often go awry, but
it takes him thirty lines to say it and his speech is so full of
difficult words and farfetched analogies that it resembles the
object of his own knotty metaphor:

> checks and disasters
> Grow in the veins of actions highest rear'd,
> As knots, by the conflux of meeting sap,

Infects the sound pine, and diverts his grain
Tortive and errant from his course of growth.

[I.iii.5]

The situation Agamemnon is addressing himself to is one that has gotten beyond men's control: the war goes tediously on, his ranks are disordered, the event never matches expectation (or, as he terms it, "that unbodied figure of the thought / That gave't surmised shape"). And his language expresses the effort and difficulty of dealing with that situation. It is an excessive language—excessively long, excessively difficult—as if Agamemnon were aware that all the words in the world can still not account for things as they are. It is a verbal assault, an attempt to order, through language, a situation inherently lacking in order.[1]

Agamemnon's lieutenants do little better. Nestor manages to load the most art onto the least matter; as if Agamemnon's thirty tortuous lines were not enough, Nestor must be his seconder:

With due observance of thy godlike seat,
Great Agamemnon, Nestor shall apply
Thy latest words.

[I.iii.31]

His application shows that faint defect of age, garrulity; it is full of mythological personifications which tend more to confuse than to clarify the issue:

But let the ruffian Boreas once enrage
The gentle Thetis, and anon behold
The strong-ribb'd bark through liquid mountains cut,

1. The conflict in styles throughout the play, and the difficulty of (especially) Greek public rhetoric, are recognized by A. S. Knowland, "*Troilus and Cressida*," *Shakespeare Quarterly* 10 (Summer 1959): 353–65. Like Knowland, I disagree with Una Ellis-Fermor's opinion that Agamemnon and Nestor speak a language that is "virile" and appropriate to its context. But see her excellent chapter on the play in *The Frontiers of Drama* (New York, 1946).

Bounding between the two moist elements
Like Perseus' horse.

[I.iii.38]

Ulysses has the good fortune to strike off a speech that has become a standard text on the Elizabethan World Picture. But in the context of the play his words are as ironically ineffectual as Agamemnon's or Nestor's. For it is not, as it turns out, Ulysses's speech which alters the course of events; the quite unexpected appearance of Aeneas, rather, bringing with him Hector's challenge, holds the promise of a break in the sprawling stalemate. Ulysses's words, from any practical point of view, are spent in vain, and even his succeeding effort to manage events—his plan to shame Achilles into action—will prove irrelevant to the actual outcome. When Achilles does rearm, it will be for a reason quite apart from Ulysses's intent; it will be the result of a moment's passion, a chance occurrence, which will give one more proof of the inadequacy of words (Greek or Trojan) to engage the real situation effectively.

Thus from the very outset of *Troilus and Cressida,* and on both sides of its war, we find those expressive difficulties which inaugurate the Shakespearean tragic moment. In *Titus Andronicus* we first saw the imperative to speak, and the great difficulty of its fulfilling. In *Hamlet* we found that the condition which deprived the hero of an adequate expressive mode involved the lack of commensurate values. Now, in *Troilus and Cressida,* too, the lack of commensurate values is apparent; and with the Trojans' debate (II.ii), where the question is specifically one of values, the lack of commensurates is so apparent that Elsinore seems, by comparison, a government by consensus.

The distance between the participants in the debate is put for us in mathematical terms. Hector, who finds "modest doubt" to be "The beacon of the wise," thinks Helen is not worth the losses incurred for her. He speaks in terms of *tenths, tithes,* of *one in ten.* Hector determines values by subtraction and division, for the values he perceives are derivable according to a common calculus:

> Let Helen go.
> Since the first sword was drawn about this question,
> Every tithe soul 'mongst many thousand dismes
> Hath been as dear as Helen—I mean, of ours.
> If we have lost so many tenths of ours
> To guard a thing not ours, nor worth to us,
> Had it our name, the value of one ten,
> What merit's in that reason which denies
> The yielding of her up?
>
> [II.ii.17]

But Troilus rejects the entire principle of measurement: like Hamlet converting Gertrude's "common" into his own very different "Ay, 'tis common," Troilus brushes aside any objective measurement that conflicts with his subjective evaluation. He has nothing to do with finite arithmetic, and sets objective demonstration at nought in comparison with "that within which passes" demonstration:

> Fie, fie, my brother!
> Weigh you the worth and honour of a king,
> So great as our dread father's, in a scale
> Of common ounces? Will you with counters sum
> The past-proportion of his infinite,
> And buckle in a waist most fathomless
> With spans and inches so diminutive
> As fears and reasons? Fie, for godly shame!
>
> [II.ii.25]

The distance between Hector and Troilus is absolute. To Hector's "Brother, she is not worth what she doth cost / The keeping," comes Troilus's affirmation of pure subjectivity, "What's aught but as 'tis valued?" (II.ii.51).

So diverse are the brothers' points of view that the scene is really less a debate—a dialectical procedure requiring at least some common ground to begin on—than it is a demonstration

of the impossibility of communication where common values
are lacking. Hector's turnabout is proof of this, for his capitu-
lation to Troilus has nothing, finally, to do with any of the
arguments advanced. Hector abandons his position immediately after giving it his strongest support; there is no "reason"
for his reversal: the "moral laws / Of nature and of nations
speak aloud" in favor of returning Helen; the most fundamental ethical principles demand a settlement for peace:

> Thus to persist
> In doing wrong extenuates not wrong,
> But makes it much more heavy.
> [II.ii.186]

"Hector's opinion / Is this, in way of truth." What then but
weariness over a debate in which neither side can understand
the other makes Hector suddenly declare, "My spritely brethren, I propend to you / In resolution to keep Helen still"?
"Reason" and objective values remain unaltered, but so too do
the subjectivist's rallying points, "our joint and several digni-
ties": there is no possibility of mediating between them.

For the audience, therefore, the point of the debate scene
lies less in our own determination of value—in whether we
find Hector or Troilus more convincing—than in the dramatic
situation itself. This scene, like the Greek council in Act I, is
indeed "closely packed with thought," but that need not imply
(as W. W. Lawrence argues) "that [the] dramatic value is
seriously impaired." [2] The clotted thought in both instances
is part of the "dramatic value": it is the dramatization of linguistic inadequacy in the face of a situation intrinsically confused and deprived of the possibility of resolution. Hector's
sudden turnabout in the question of Helen's return is emblematic of the only sort of action this world is able to sustain
—action unreasonable, lacking in preparation, contrary to
expectation; action which resolves none of the play-world's
deeply divisive problems.

2. W. W. Lawrence, *Shakespeare's Problem Comedies* (New York, 1931),
p. 172.

Thus we have, abundantly, in *Troilus and Cressida,* the pre-conditions for tragedy. But the characteristic pattern of action is blocked: ironic dissolution is allowed to have its way over heroic reintegration. The play looks like a tragedy or, rather, as if it were going to *become* a tragedy; but confusion only gives way to greater confusion as each attempt at clarification—in council and debate scenes and in lovers' speeches—takes the situation farther along the road to the unformed and chaotic.

We shall have to trace this process of ironic disintegration in greater detail, but perhaps enough has already been said for us to pause now and attempt some generic classification more precise than "problem play." And the clue we must follow is precisely this matter of the frustration of esthetic expectation. From the very outset of the play, with the conflict between what the Prologue promises and what we actually find in the play, we have been confronted with a tension between an ideal of form and a quite different reality of content. By remarking on the appropriateness of his bearing to the theme at hand, the Prologue implies an ideal of decorum. Indeed he goes further: with his promise that the play "Leaps o'er the vaunt and firstlings of those broils, / Beginning in the middle; starting thence away / To what may be digested in a play," the Prologue introduces an echo of the Horatian formula for the well-made epic:

> semper ad eventum festinat et in medias res
> non secus ac notas auditorem rapit, et quae
> desperat tractata nitescere posse, relinquit,
> atque ita mentitur, sic veris falsa remiscet,
> primo ne medium, medio ne discrepet imum.

> ["Ever he hastens to the issue, and hurries his hearer into the story's midst, as if already known, and what he fears he cannot make attractive to his touch he abandons; and so skilfully does he invent, so closely does he blend fact and fiction, that the middle is not discordant with the beginning, nor the end with the middle."] [3]

3. *Ars Poetica*, ll. 148–52; Loeb Library ed., pp. 462–63.

The examples Horace adduces are drawn from the Troy
legend, increasing the likelihood that, although epic and not
drama is the subject, Shakespeare was actually recalling the
passage from the *Ars Poetica* in his Prologue. But how poorly,
even allowing for the differences between epic and drama, has
Shakespeare followed the stylistic ideal, especially in the matter of abandoning what cannot be made attractive: the in-
tractability of his material in *Troilus and Cressida,* his failure
to dramatize, and his excessive reliance on undramatic speeches
are precisely the commonplace criticisms made of the play.

But it is also possible to see this contradiction between the
ideal of form and the actual content of the play, not as an
artistic failure, but as a positive principle of Shakespeare's
dramaturgy. For this contradiction between formal expectation and actual content suggests the nature of a parody, and
parody, it seems to me, is the best word to describe this most
peculiar of plays. Parody, as distinct from satire, is intimately
a matter of the mimesis itself, rather than of an attitude toward the objects of mimesis; it "derides, not its subject, but a
particular literary work or style, by imitating its features and
applying them to trivial or grossly discordant materials." [4]

In *Troilus and Cressida,* tragedy—the form and what that

4. M. H. Abrams, *A Glossary of Literary Terms* (New York, 1957), p. 10.
Since Oscar J. Campbell's designation, "comicall satyre," comes fairly
close to my own sense of the play, it may seem an unnecessary com-
plication to bedevil it with yet another generic label. But Campbell's Jon-
sonian terminology is misleading, since it implies (what in fact Campbell
believed) that Shakespeare was attacking "social follies and ethical lapses,"
and therefore "made the play a vehicle for his political philosophy"
(*Comicall Satyre and Shakespeare's "Troilus and Cressida"* [San Marino,
Calif., 1938], pp. 185, 234). I agree, rather, with Alvin Kernan that *"Troilus
and Cressida* is not finally a satiric play . . . [because] it is not in the end
an attack on any specific attitudes or modes of conduct" (*The Cankered
Muse* [New Haven, 1959], p. 197). I am using "parody" as a structural
term; it does not necessarily imply that the play is funny. Certainly I cannot agree with Alice Walker (ed., New Cambridge *Troilus and Cressida*
[Cambridge, 1957]) that the play is all comedy, and that even such a scene
as that of the killing of Hector is meant to be risible (cf. p. xxix of
her edition).

form implies about man's ability to transcend his world through an artistic ordering of it—is the burden of Shakespeare's parody. The conditions for tragedy are present, and our expectations are aroused for a work in the high tragical vein, but with the very first speeches—those of the romantic Troilus, the vulgar Pandarus, the long-winded Agamemnon— we are confronted with "grossly discordant materials." The gross discord interacts with the formal ideal to produce a different reality, a countervision or antitragedy, which marks the play out as parody—deadly serious, but parody nonetheless.

One indication of the parodic nature of the play comes from the overt instances of parody or satire (it is not always possible to maintain the distinction strictly) by the characters in the play. It is remarkable how frequently the war between Trojan and Greek—or between Trojan and Trojan, Greek and Greek —dwindles into attacks between rival parodists. Thersites, of course, is the most consistent, indeed the most professional, parodist of them all. But more revealing than the outright Thersitical attack (which is usually strictly satiric) are the instances of Thersites's participation in the parodic game frequently played by the characters. In Act III, scene 3, Thersites stages "the pageant of Ajax": "I will put on his presence" (269), Thersites says, and with Patroclus as interlocutor he proceeds to parody the beef-witted soldier. His technique is the obvious one of exaggeration, or caricature: Thersites's Ajax speaks in monosyllabic expletives and irrelevant and unwitty witticisms. This parodic attack on Ajax is more effective than the ordinary Thersitical onslaught, for Thersites, by effacing himself and appropriating the "presence" of his adversary, makes Ajax dwindle into an unimpressive object of laughter.

Thersites, precisely because he is a professional satirist, is not, for our purpose, the most interesting example of a parodist-within-the-parody. He is only doing what we would expect him to do; it is more significant to notice that amateurs turn parodist as well. In Act I, scene 3, Aeneas appears with a message for Agamemnon; unwittingly addressing the object of his search, he asks, "May one that is a herald and a prince / Do a

fair message to his [Agamemnon's] kingly eyes?"(218). Agamemnon's reply is somewhat fulsome (though, to be sure, no
more so than Aeneas's question), and Aeneas now continues the
exchange in a manner worthy of the Ancient Pistol:

> *Aene.*   How may
> A stranger to those most imperial looks
> Know them from eyes of other mortals?
> *Agam.*   How?
> *Aene.* Ay;
> I ask, that I might waken reverence,
> And bid the cheek be ready with a blush
> Modest as Morning when she coldly eyes
> The youthful Phoebus.
> Which is that god in office, guiding men?
> Which is the high and mighty Agamemnon?
>   [I.iii.223]

Conceivably, Aeneas does not intend the question as mockery,
but Agamemnon, at least, suspects a parodist's intent: "This
Troyan scorns us, or the men of Troy / Are ceremonious
courtiers" (I.iii.233). Intentional or not, it would appear that
social exchanges in this world so frequently verge on the parodic that Aeneas's flattery is immediately felt, by his hearers,
to be a parody.

Achilles and Patroclus, who were respectively audience and
straightman for Thersites's "pageant of Ajax," are themselves
frequent parodists. But Shakespeare, in a manner that is
typical of his handling of the play-within-a-play idea, holds an
extra mirror up to the nature within, and gives us our best
view of Achilles and Patroclus in Ulysses's parody of *them*. The
situation in Act 1, scene 3 (ll. 142 ff.) is complex: Ulysses paro-
dies Achilles and Patroclus parodying the audience Ulysses is
speaking to. The wily Ulysses thus has it both ways: the actors
and the stage-audience alike become the objects of his scath-
ing imitations. The passage is worth quoting at length, because
in its specific reference to theatrical modes it provides an excellent adumbration of the way in which *Troilus and Cressida*

as a whole functions as a parody of tragic attitudes and tragic structure:

> The great Achilles, whom opinion crowns
> The sinew and the forehand of our host,
> Having his ear full of his airy fame,
> Grows dainty of his worth, and in his tent
> Lies *mocking our designs;* with him Patroclus
> Upon a lazy bed the livelong day
> *Breaks scurril jests;*
> *And with ridiculous and awkward action—*
> *Which, slanderer, he imitation calls—*
> *He pageants us.* Sometime, great Agamemnon,
> Thy topless deputation he puts on;
> And *like a strutting player whose conceit*
> *Lies in his hamstring, and doth think it rich*
> *To hear the wooden dialogue and sound*
> *'Twixt his stretch'd footing and the scaffoldage—*
> *Such to-be-pitied and o'er wrested seeming*
> *He acts thy greatness in;* and when he speaks
> 'Tis like a chime a-mending; with *terms unsquar'd,*
> Which, from the tongue of roaring Typhon dropp'd,
> Would seem *hyperboles.* At this fusty stuff
> The large Achilles, on his press'd bed lolling,
> From his deep chest *laughs out a loud applause;*
> Cries 'Excellent! 'tis Agamemnon just.
> Now *play me Nestor;* hem, and stroke thy beard,
> As he being drest to some oration'.
> That's done—as near as the extremest ends
> Of parallels, as like as Vulcan and his wife;
> Yet god Achilles still cries 'Excellent!
> 'Tis Nestor right. *Now play him* me, Patroclus,
> Arming to answer in a night alarm'.
> And then, forsooth, the faint defects of age
> Must be the *scene of mirth:* to cough and spit
> And, with a palsy-fumbling on his gorget,
> Shake in and out the rivet. And at this sport

Sir Valour dies; cries 'O, enough Patroclus;
Or give me ribs of steel! I shall split all
In pleasure of my spleen'. And in this fashion
All our abilities, gifts, natures, shapes,
Severals and generals of grace exact,
Achievements, orders, plots, preventions,
Excitements to the field or speech for truce,
Success or loss, what is or is not, serves
As *stuff for these two to make paradoxes.*
                                   [I.iii.142; italics mine]

"Scurril jests," "ridiculous and awkward action— / Which,
slanderer, he imitation calls": on a greatly magnified scale, and
with an intense seriousness of purpose, this is a fair estimate
of Shakespeare's technique throughout the play. As Ulysses
knows—and his knowledge is what gives the speech its wonder-
fully sly humor—Patroclus's parody comes devastatingly close
to the truth. This very scene has begun with Agamemnon's
tortuous address on the "checks and disasters that / Grow in
the veins of actions highest rear'd," a speech indeed full (as
Ulysses says of the Patroclus version) of "terms unsquar'd,"
"hyperboles," and "fusty stuff." Nestor, described by the parodists as hemming and stroking his beard "as . . . being drest
to some oration," has similarly shown, *in propria persona,* that
the parodic version has caught the man aright.

The Greeks hardly need Patroclus to make "paradoxes" of
their "achievements, plots, orders, preventions": their own
overelaborate and finally ineffectual and irrelevant public
rhetoric achieves that without help. And were Achilles and
Patroclus to leave their "press'd bed" long enough to observe
the Trojan scene as well as the Greek, they could no doubt
find rich material for parody within Troy too. For (as we have
seen) the discordant voices in the Trojan camp similarly stand
as self-parodies: Troilus's hectic romanticism becomes ridiculous when paired with Pandarus's cynical prose, while
Hector's rational sentences on value become (in light of his
own irrational support of Troilus), like the "o'er-wrested

seeming" of Ulysses's "strutting player," a kind of sound and fury signifying nothing.

A wide variety of special languages is tried—the language of public oration (Agamemnon's and Nestor's), of romantic love and war-lust (Troilus's), of cool reason (Hector's), even a language that can parody them all (Ulysses's)—but none proves entirely effective in the immediate circumstances. All the major characters, the Greeks in their way and the Trojans in theirs, act their "greatness" with the "to-be-pitied" dramatic incompetence (not to be confused with incompetence on Shakespeare's part) which Ulysses describes. None of the characters finds a rhetoric adequate to the situation; and each of them, in his attempt to act his own version of the heroic manner, increases the tension between the formal ideal and the actual evolved content, marking the play out, not as a tragedy, but as a parody of the tragic.

The actions of the play—its language of gesture—mock the tragic ideal as surely as do the words. Tragedy, as we have seen, typically proceeds to some consummating action, to the gesture which enables language; but in *Troilus and Cressida* it is the lack of action, the irresoluteness and attenuation of gesture, which is most notable. And here, starting at the most general level of action, there is something very curious; for while there is division within the Greek camp and division within Troy, the lack of real division *between* Greece and Troy is the force that is, dramatically, pulling the play away from tragedy toward parody. There is, of course, a war—a long, tedious, costly war of attrition—but the play takes place during a period of truce. Greeks enter Troy and Trojans enter the Greek camp easily and frequently, and there is a generally depressing (or ironic) effect in this familarity between the two armies. The hostility between the camps dwindles to a show of verbal abuse. The crisis point for tragedy has long ago been reached, but the absence of any great action attenuates that point until a peevish ennui takes the place of tragic conflict.

There are, no doubt, differences between the Greeks and the Trojans: there is comparatively more "cynicism" on the one

side and "romanticism" on the other; but these hardly consti-
tute polarities. I cannot find in the play that sharp distinction
G. Wilson Knight perceives: "The Trojan party," he writes,
"stands for human beauty and worth, the Greek party for the
bestial and stupid elements of man." [5] Pandarus, after all, is a
Trojan; and one may at least feel some qualms about the "human beauty" of Troilus's devotion to continuing the war. As
important as the similarity between individuals on the two
sides is the blurring effect of the frequent commerce between
them, a commerce which carries the dramatic suggestion that
the two nations might equally well be living together as fight-
ing one another. The two most notable instances of commerce
between the camps, the exchange of Cressida and the "sportful
combat" between Hector and Ajax—dramatically, two of the
central actions of the play—emphasize the closeness of the
parties rather than any polarity.

The greeting (IV.i) between the agents in Cressida's exchange—Diomedes for the Greeks and Aeneas for the Trojans
—indicates this lack of real opposition. The two men are
courteous, indeed courtly; they declare that they will love each
other during the truce but hate again in war. But their love
and hatred are closely, strangely, blended. Aeneas, swearing by
the hand of his mother whom (according to legend) Diomedes
had wounded, declares:

> By Venus' hand I swear
> No man alive can love in such a sort
> The thing he means to kill, more excellently.
>   [IV.i.24]

Diomedes can reciprocate the emotional oxymoron: "We sym-
pathise," he says. Paris, observing the greetings, sums up their
curiously ambivalent tone: "This is the most despiteful'st
gentle greeting, / The noblest hateful love, that e'er I heard
of" (IV.i.34).

Paris himself has nothing but kind words for Diomedes; he
even expresses real interest in Diomedes's opinion of the war:

5. *The Wheel of Fire*, 4th ed. revised and enlarged (London, 1949),
p. 47.

And tell me, noble Diomed—faith, tell me true,
Even in the soul of sound good-fellowship—
Who in your thoughts deserves fair Helen best,
Myself or Menelaus?

[IV.i.53]

Under the circumstances—men have been dying in a war over his "fair Helen," after all—it is difficult to say whether Paris's notion of "good-fellowship" is less depressing than Diomedes's cynical reply:

Both alike:
He merits well to have her that doth seek her,
Not making any scruple of her soilure,
With such a hell of pain and world of charge;
And you as well to keep her that defend her,
Not palating the taste of her dishonour,
With such a costly loss of wealth and friends.

[IV.i.56]

Diomedes is of Thersites's opinion: on one side is the "cuckold," on the other the "lecher," and "Both merits pois'd, each weighs nor less nor more: / But he as he, the heavier for a whore" (IV.i.67).

The blend of love and hate expressed in the ambivalent greeting between Diomedes and Aeneas now gives way to an understandable disgust. To Paris's tame comment, "You are too bitter to your countrywoman," comes Diomedes's uncompromising reply:

She's bitter to her country. Hear me, Paris:
For every false drop in her bawdy veins
A Grecian's life hath sunk; for every scruple
Of her contaminated carrion weight
A Troyan hath been slain; since she could speak,
She hath not given so many good words breath
As for her Greeks and Troyans suff'red death.

[IV.i.70]

Diomedes's outburst, with its juxtaposition of a very palpable "death" to the mere "breath" of Helen's "good words," exposes the fatuity of the preceding oxymoronic greetings. No one's words in this world can counterpoise that heavy "death."

But in the atmosphere created by such ambivalent language, it is understandable that Cressida can make her transition from Troy to Greece with such ease. Even the bawdy jokes with which the Greeks greet this daughter of the game (IV.v) are not so very different from the bawdy jokes which are the staple among Pandarus, Helen, and Paris in Troy (cf. III.i). Lust is inextricably blended with the hostility between the two camps anyway; deadly enemies express love for each other, and only a cynical disgust for the supposed cause of their enmity. The distance between Greek camp and Trojan citadel is small enough, in more than geographical terms, to facilitate Cressida's passage; but, ironically, that closeness leads to the opening of the real gulf which, as we will shortly see, appears in the world of the play—the impassable gulf Troilus is to find gaping within his own soul.

The other great action (or, as it turns out, non-action), the combat between the Greek and Trojan champions, has about it the same air of irresolution, lack of true opposites, and anti-climax which the exchange of Cressida has. Hector announces his plan at the end of the Trojan debate scene (II.ii), just after his bewildering turnabout in the argument over value. His challenge, Hector makes clear, is intended to be something decisive, a total change from the tedious business of the truce:

> I have a roisting challenge sent amongst
> The dull and factious nobles of the Greeks
> Will strike amazement to their drowsy spirits.
> [II.ii.208]

But, as if to underscore the ironic disparity between intent and actuality, Shakespeare has already let us hear that challenge, given by Aeneas in Act I, scene 3, and we thus know that the great meeting which is intended to shake the rust off "this dull and long-continued truce" is but another example of love and hate curiously, irresolutely, bound together. Hec-

tor's challenge, as announced to the Greeks by Aeneas, is to
the man

> That holds his honour higher than his ease,
> That seeks his praise more than he fears his peril,
> That knows his valour and knows not his fear,
> That loves his mistress more than in confession
> With truant vows to her own lips he loves,
> And dare avow her beauty and her worth
> In other arms than hers. . . .
>
> [I.iii.266]

From the first, then, the combat is set up as a romantic spectacle, a game, based in part on the old wordplay between two
sorts of "arms," which can prove nothing more than that
Hector "hath a lady wiser, fairer, truer, / Than ever Greek
did couple in his arms" (275). For the Greeks (hardly stricken
with the intended amazement) the combat becomes an opportunity, not for romantic indulgence but for cunning. Although everyone knows that the challenge is meant for Achilles, Ulysses has a better idea: the blockish Ajax will fight in
Achilles's place. If Ajax wins, it "will physic the great Myrmi-
don," Achilles, of his pride; if Ajax loses, "Yet go we under
our opinion still / That we have better men" (I.iii.378, 383).

The substitution of Ajax makes the "sportful combat" (as
Ulysses calls it, I.iii.335) an emblem for the entire action of the
play. The fight is abortive from the start, its mighty opposites
no opposites at all. For, as Aeneas says, "This Ajax is half
made of Hector's blood"—he is Hector's cousin, Priam's
nephew—and in deference to the relationship, "half Hector
stays at home":

> Half heart, half hand, half Hector comes to seek
> This blended knight, half Troyan and half Greek.
>
> [IV.v.83]

The lack of real opposition builds anticlimax into the very
attempt at action: "The combatants being kin / Half stints

their strife before their strokes begin" (IV.v.92). The irresolute blend of love and hate expressed in the uneasy oxymorons at Cressida's exchange becomes, in this combat, an action-
defeating blood-relationship. The combat ends before it has
really begun, so that (as Aeneas says) "There is expectance
here from both the sides / What further you will do." Hector's answer "is embracement" (IV.v.146).

Now "embracement" is the proper issue of tragic conflict,
but not this sort of embracement. For the "issue" here resolves
nothing; it is an unearned embracement which still leaves the
oxymoronic love-hate in perilous balance. The combat thus
mirrors, at the level of a ritualized action, the linguistic failures we have noticed. The "sportful combat," a virtually
mock-heroic meeting, is, in its irrelevance to the dramatic
outcome of the play, another parody of tragic conflict.

Indeed, the inability to find a ritual that is not inconclusive or rendered meaningless by subsequent events, marks the
play's action out as the antithesis of tragedy. The perverted
gesture and the inadequate word are the effects (as Hamlet,
for instance, found) of being-in-time; history is an endless
series of such unplanned obsolescences. Being-in-time, the condition Ulysses describes with such depressing accuracy, is the
unregenerate condition tragedy would confront and answer.
The completed tragic action should be immune to time's
"rich thievery." But in *Troilus and Cressida* nothing is immune.

The pagan setting of the play, and its apparently unchris-
tian concern with love and honor, ought not to blind us to
its typically Renaissance concern with, and horror at, mutability. *Mutability* is the Spenserian word; *Time* is, in *Troilus
and Cressida,* the Shakespearean word; both are related to
what I have called history. Troilus is not the only character
in the play who would have reason to exclaim with Spenser,
"O, pitious worke of Mutabilitie"; as their speeches in Act
III, scene 2 emphasize, the very names of Cressida and Pandarus stand as object lessons in the effects of Time; and
Ulysses no less than Hector finds what it means to try to act in

"this state of life so tickle" (*F.Q.*, VII.viii.1.6).[6] *Troilus and Cressida* is the nightmare version of the world Spenser dreamed: here Mutability *is* the ultimate reality, and things do not turn "to themselves at length againe" to work "their owne perfection" (*F.Q.*, VII.vii.58.6). Time is the all-devouring medium of *Troilus and Cressida:* there are no "pillours of eternity, / That is contrayr to Mutabilitie" (*F.Q.*, end).

Ulysses gives us our fullest image of a historical world deprived of the possibility of a renovating End: "Time hath, my lord, a wallet at his back, / Wherein he puts alms for oblivion" (III.iii.145). This is the secular world—both in the sense of *worldly* and of *indefinitely long-lasting*—which makes mockery of our "good deeds past" and promises for the future only that "fine revolution" which Hamlet traced in Alexander's progress to a bunghole. Man, as he is found in Ulysses's speech on time, runs a perpetual race and must keep on running simply to stay upright on his treadmill; to pause for an instant is to have emulation's "thousand sons" "all rush by / And leave you hindmost," or to be a fallen horse in the "first rank," which lies as "pavement to the abject rear" (III.iii.159, 161). Time rushes on and man must rush with it, not in the impossible hope of passing it, but simply to keep his footing:

> Perseverance, dear my lord,
> Keeps honour bright. To have done is to hang
> Quite out of fashion, like a rusty mail
> In monumental mock'ry.
>
> [III.iii.150]

While Ulysses is the philosophical spokesman for the secular, he is far from being alone in his view of the world. Cressida, for instance, although hardly a philosopher, has a similar opinion of what it means "to have done":

> Women are angels, wooing:
> Things won are done; joy's soul lies in the doing.

6. Spenser, *The Complete Poetical Works,* ed. R. E. Neil Dodge (Cambridge, Mass., 1908).

> That she belov'd knows nought that knows not this:
> Men prize the thing ungain'd more than it is.
> That she was never yet that ever knew
> Love got so sweet as when desire did sue;
> Therefore this maxim out of love I teach:
> Achievement is command; ungain'd, beseech.
>
> [I.ii.278]

If Ulysses's lesson is lost on Achilles, Cressida knows and acts on it by instinct: Troilus is the "parting guest" of Ulysses's metaphor (III.iii.165 ff.), Diomedes "the comer" whom Cressida, like a proper child of Time, will welcome smilingly.

Even the romantic Troilus gives us an image of the world as perpetual time-progression. The following speech (his counterpart to Cressida's jingle about wooing), although it seems at first to contrast so strikingly in tone with Cressida's cynicism, actually expresses equally with Cressida's speech a fear of ending—of consummation, in every sense of the word—which is the mark of the world-in-time:

> I am giddy; expectation whirls me round.
> Th' imaginary relish is so sweet
> That it enchants my sense; what will it be
> When that the wat'ry palate tastes indeed
> Love's thrice-repured nectar? Death, I fear me;
> Swooning destruction; or some joy too fine,
> Too subtle-potent, tun'd too sharp in sweetness,
> For the capacity of my ruder powers.
> I fear it much; and I do fear besides
> That I shall lose distinction in my joys;
> As doth a battle, when they charge on heaps
> The enemy flying.
>
> [III.ii.17]

Troilus's brilliant, breathless picture of sexuality provides a fitting image of the paradoxical effects of action in a world dominated by time. To *do* is to run the risk of attaining, which means, in history or in orgasm, to *have done*. Troilus's romanticism thus gives us the same world as Ulysses's and

Cressida's cynicism, where to keep on going and never to arrive is the only alternative to being crushed into formless dissolution by the horses of time. Different as they are, both Ulysses and Troilus inhabit the same world of inevitable self-defeat, and it is entirely appropriate that Troilus, in his leave-taking of Cressida, should echo Ulysses's imagery ("Injurious time now with a robber's haste / Crams his rich thievery up, he knows not how," [IV.iv.41]), and that Ulysses should be the guide in Troilus's descent into the hell of his own soul.

The dominance of unregenerate time appears in imagery throughout the play. Garrulous, ineffectual Nestor is called a "good old chronicle" who walks "hand in hand with time" (IV.v.202). Although Hector expresses his faith that "The end crowns all; / And that old common arbitrator, Time, / Will one day end it" (IV.v.224), the emphasis falls upon the far-off, indefinite "one day" rather than upon any real eschatological hope; and this emphasis is increased by Ulysses's almost weary reply, "So to him we leave it." Indeed, the tone of the play is set by Agamemnon's speech in Act I, which in its tortuous language is a demonstration as well as a definition of the problem. Agamemnon speaks of how

> The ample proposition that hope makes
> In all designs begun on earth below
> Fails in the promis'd largeness.
>
> [I.iii.3]

The lesson history teaches, Agamemnon says, is that "every action" is drawn "bias and thwart" from the imagined purpose which "gave't surmised shape." It is the failure of action to correspond to intention which has "set these jaundies" in the Grecian cheeks, but Agamemnon now assures them that such failures are the inevitable way of the world, are indeed "But the protractive trials of great Jove / To find persistive constancy in men" (I.iii.20). And persistive constancy is the one possible virtue in a world where the crowning End is only More of the Same.

The extent and meaning of Shakespeare's parody of tragic

structure becomes apparent in light of this insistent secularity. The great tragedies seek a creation beyond the ravishing effects of time, a culminating action, like Titus's "device . . . to make us wonder'd at," which infuses the past with meaning. In a book whose very title, *The Sense of an Ending*, is pertinent to the present study, Frank Kermode has traced "the paradigms of apocalypse" in world literature; as Kermode points out, the desire for a history that would be redeemed through its relationship to a significant End is deeply embedded in the Western tradition. In the Renaissance, tragedy became the heir to the Christian apocalyptic tradition: "Apocalypse, which succeeded prophecy, merges with tragedy; the humble elect survive not all the kings of the earth as in Revelation, but the one king whose typical story in enacted before them." [7] The end of *King Lear* makes the juncture between apocalypse and tragedy explicit: "Is this the promis'd end? / Or image of that horror?"

But in *Troilus and Cressida* the promise is indefinitely delayed. History cannot be redeemed; all we are left with are the formless husks of oblivion. Action is swept away in the rush of time, and "time the destroyer" is not "time the preserver." Troilus wins and loses Cressida in one instant: she is lost to him even before the exchange, lost at the instant of consummation, since to *do* is to *have done*. "How my achievements mock me!" (IV.ii.69): Troilus's despairing comment sums up the inevitable effects of action in a world dominated by Time.

What is true of action is also true of formal expression. Attempts at simple intelligibility are doomed in a world where the ever-encroaching future swallows up the tenuous present, "with a robber's haste." The specious subtleties and tortured rhetoric of both Greek and Trojan public language are gambits designed to wrest some meaning from a world successively rendered meaningless by the movement of time. Ritualized actions especially, which depend for their significance upon the relevance of all such past actions, become mere empty forms

7. *The Sense of an Ending* (New York, 1967), pp. 28, 30.

that leave the participants with "expectance" rather than fulfillment. The ever-changing reality makes the most elaborate of plans irrelevant at the moment of their intended fruition. Ritualized encounters change meaning as they are acted out. Words and gestures alike are inconclusive, equally prey to all-devouring time.

And the most solemn of oaths, made in the name of history itself, are broken. The "end" comes for Troilus as a sort of counter-ritual, a mock-tragic close, which compromises a terrifying parody of apocalypse not unlike the end of Pope's *Dunciad*. The scene in which Troilus finds ocular proof of Cressida's infidelity (V.ii) is highly ritualized; indeed, as we may have come to expect, it is virtually a play-within-the-play, with Cressida and Diomedes as actors, Troilus and Ulysses as audience, and Thersites as ironic chorus. Troilus watches the scene unfold with a growing horror that can be controlled only by denying his very nature: "I will not be myself," he tells the anxious Ulysses, "nor have cognition / Of what I feel" (62).

What he sees is the profanation of the vows he and Cressida have sworn; the visible sign of that "pledge," Troilus's sleeve, is transferred to Diomedes, and thus this most decisive action of the play comes as a parodic version of the ceremony Troilus had believed was inviolable. When this counter-ritual is completed, and Troilus's Cressida has become Diomedes's Cressida, Ulysses pronounces the *consummatum est* which belongs to every tragic action: "All's done, my lord" (113). But this consummation, like the "embracement" which ended the combat between Hector and Ajax, is the opposite of that consummation the tragic hero devoutly wishes; it is, rather, the realization of his worst fears of the effects of ending in the world-in-time.

In Shakespearean tragedy, the consummation of the hero's agony is followed by the survivors' retrospective efforts to understand what has been enacted before them. They look back upon the anatomy of their society which the tragic action has revealed, and forward to a life renovated by the patterns

they can discover. In *Troilus and Cressida,* this critical effort is
left to Troilus himself. When Ulysses asks why he stays after
the spectacle is over, Troilus responds, "To make a recordation to my soul / Of every syllable that here was spoke" (114).
But that recordation, which in tragedy affirms the reuniting
of society on ruins that have now been made foundations, presents in Troilus's parodic version an image of chaos, of meaninglessness, of the horror of ends which are no real ends at
all.

What Troilus has seen impugns the very possibility of
meaningful utterance. If what was once, was—if Troilus and
Cressida loved—then what is now cannot be: "But if I tell
how these two did coact, / Shall I not lie in publishing a
truth?" (V.ii.116). To save the truth of the past, Troilus must
deny the present; he must deny "th' attest of eyes and ears"
which in their "deceptious functions" would have him believe that time can empty vows (words whose function is to
affirm the truth of words) of the meanings upon which he has
rested his own being. If Troilus is to remain Troilus, then
the Cressida he has seen cannot be Troilus's Cressida:

> This she? No; this is Diomed's Cressida.
> If beauty have a soul, this is not she;
> If souls guide vows, if vows be sanctimonies,
> If sanctimony be the gods' delight,
> If there be rule in unity itself,
> This was not she.
>
> [V.ii.135]

Without the "rule in unity"—that what is, is itself and
nothing else—the only rule is chaos. The intellectual bases
for rational discourse are gone:

> O madness of discourse,
> That cause sets up with and against itself!
> Bifold authority! where reason can revolt
> Without perdition, and loss assume all reason
> Without revolt: this is, and is not, Cressid.
>
> [V.ii.140]

In place of the resolving close of tragedy, there comes for
Troilus the terrible intuition of a soul and a world deprived
of all cohesion. Put though it is in strenuously paradoxical
terms, Troilus's agony is a psychologically profound study of
a sensibility becoming most violently dissociated:

> Within my soul there doth conduce a fight
> Of this strange nature, that a thing inseparate
> Divides more wider than the sky and earth;
> And yet the spacious breadth of this division
> Admits no orifex for a point as subtle
> As Ariachne's broken woof to enter.
>
> [V.ii.145]

In the Trojan council scene in Act II, scene 2, we saw an
early instance of discourse failing in the conflict of two irreconcilable truths. There, the conflict between Hector's objective and Troilus's subjective valuations deprived the Trojans of the commensurate terms necessary for fulfilled communication. By Act V, that conflict has invaded Troilus's soul;
but even as early as Act II we had a foreshadowing of the
direction the play would take. There, in his speech in favor
of subjective valuation, Troilus draws an analogy that finds
terrifying realization in Act V:

> I take to-day a wife, and my election
> Is led on in the conduct of my will;
> My will enkindled by mine eyes and ears,
> Two traded pilots 'twixt the dangerous shores
> Of will and judgment: how may I avoid,
> Although my will distaste what it elected,
> The wife I chose? There can be no evasion
> To blench from this and to stand firm by honour.
>
> [II.ii.61]

Now it is precisely in this hypothetical matter of "the wife
I chose" that Troilus finds his "eyes and ears" unable to navi-
gate between "the dangerous shores / Of will and judgment."
Unable, by the very terms of honor he himself has set up, "to
blench" from his choice, but equally unable to deny the evi-

dence of objective reality (as, earlier, Hector and Troilus between them had been unable to mediate the two), Troilus is
forced to recognize the dissolution of that world whose in-
stability the audience has seen from the play's beginning.

"The bonds of heaven are slipp'd, dissolv'd, and loos'd"
(V.ii.154), and now Degree, the cosmic principle of order described by Ulysses in Act I, is "shaked" with a vengeance.
Troilus is the microcosmic image of what has become true for
the entire world of the play: the string is untuned, and only
discord follows. "Mere oppugnancy" ends the play, as force
becomes the only right, "and appetite, an universal wolf,"
makes his "universal prey" (I.iii.75–137). Troilus blames Hector for his "vice of mercy," and to Hector's remonstrance, "Fie,
savage, fie!" responds with the unvarnished, "Hector, then 'tis
wars" (V.iii.49). And why indeed should a man trouble himself with the fine points of civilized conduct? Does there not
come a letter from (as Pandarus calls her) "yond poor girl"
which proves that all is "words, words, mere words, no matter
from the heart" (V.iii. 108)?

Thersites ushers us onto the battlefield for the last time
(V.iv), and for once we may feel he speaks an almost sober
truth. The romantic plot has degenerated, as Thersites sees it,
into the "clapper-clawing" of a "young Troyan ass" and a
"Greekish whoremasterly villain" over a "dissembling luxu-
rious drab." "A th' t' other side," he says, "the policy of those
crafty swearing rascals—that stale old mouse-eaten dry cheese,
Nestor, and the same dog-fox, Ulysses—is not proved worth a
blackberry." Their "policy" has backfired: "Now is the cur
Ajax prouder than the cur Achilles, and will not arm to-day."
All the policy, the plans and speeches, of love and war, have
brought us to this scene of chaos—"Whereupon," Thersites
concludes, "the Grecians begin to proclaim barbarism, and
policy grows into an ill opinion" (V.iv.1–16).

Hector's final deed of valor is to chase "one in armor," a
mere "putrified core," like a beast for its hide. His end comes
as the most grotesque counter-ritual in the play: Achilles is
aroused at last to work—not by "policy" but by "barbarism"

—and the earlier, inconclusive ritual, staged in the full panoply of chivalric warfare between Hector and Ajax, is replayed as the murderous attack on Hector by Achilles and his Myrmidons. It is the inverted image of the sacrificial death which ends tragedy—an unsanctioned murder that gives the ironic the final triumph over the heroic. "I am unarm'd; forego this vantage, Greek" (V.iii.9): Hector's plea is pitiful in a world where rule has been swallowed in "mere oppugnancy." The deadly, silent Myrmidons surround and slay the helpless warrior, and all that is left is the fitting end to this black ritual: Hector, "at the murderer's horse's tail, / In beastly sort, dragg'd through the shameful field" (V.x.4).

"The dragon wing of night o'er-spreads the earth" (V.viii.17), and from the shade of this mock-apocalypse, this unredeeming end, Pandarus steps forth to have the last word. Troilus had called him "this sailing Pandar / Our doubtful hope, our convoy and our bark," but the dividing seas have overwhelmed Troilus; the communicative passage fails, but the poor weather-beaten vessel, Pandarus, a native to his element, remains.

Critics have complained about the inconclusive ending of *Troilus and Cressida;* from Dryden on, they have noticed that "the latter part of the tragedy is nothing but a confusion of drums and trumpets, excursions and alarms. The chief persons, who give name to the tragedy, are left alive; Cressida is false, and is not punished." [8] (Compare the comment of a modern critic: "No poetic justice is meted out to Cressida . . . [and] the elaborate plan of the Greek chiefs to shame Achilles into action misses fire completely." [9])

Considered either as tragedy or as comedy the ending *is* inconclusive. But, as Una Ellis-Fermor writes, "given discord as the central theme, it is hard to imagine how else it should formally be reflected but in a deliberately intended discord of form also." [10] That discord is the parodic version of tragedy's

8. *Essays of John Dryden,* ed. W. P. Ker, 2 vols. (Oxford, 1926), 1 : 203.
9. Lawrence, *Problem Comedies,* p. 158.
10. *Frontiers of Drama,* p. 63.

concord. A daring experiment, *Troilus and Cressida* uses the arts of language to question the efficacy of language in a secular world, uses the gestures of the stage to show man's inability to act meaningfully in a world deprived of transcendent meaning.

Of course there has to be another side to this, too; for just as the formally affirmative ending of *Hamlet* admits hints of formal inadequacy, so *Troilus and Cressida,* insofar as it is successful as drama, must contain an element of affirmation along with its denial. As Geoffrey Hartman has written (in a different context), "The reason that an artist's critique [of the bases of his art] cannot be discursive, or purely so, is that it still involves an affirmation—the new work of art." [11] Still, *Troilus and Cressida* in its overall effect remains a searching ironic parody of tragic form and tragic values—a work of high criticism which may have been, for Shakespeare, the necessary prelude to *Othello* and *Macbeth,* and to the most complex case of all, *King Lear.*

11. *Beyond Formalism* (New Haven, 1970), p. 74.

5

Othello

Sir Philip Sidney's declaration of independence for the poetic imagination, the assertion that poetry is the only "Arte deliuered to mankinde that hath not the workes of Nature for his principall obiect," is not self-evidently a defense. The poet's ability to create ex nihilo, "freely ranging onely within the Zodiack of his own wit," acknowledges in the poet vast power—but power no more assuredly divine than demonic. Perhaps Sidney realized how easily his claim could play into the hands of the Puritan opposition when he concluded the following lovely passage by noting that "these arguments wil by fewe be understood, and by fewer granted":

> Neyther let it be deemed too sawcie a comparison to ballance the highest poynt of mans wit with the efficacie of Nature: but rather giue right honor to the heauenly Maker of that maker, who, hauing made man to his owne likenes, set him beyond and ouer all the workes of that second nature, which in nothing hee sheweth so much as in Poetrie, when with the force of a diuine breath he bringeth things forth far surpassing her dooings, with no small argument to the incredulous of that first accursed fall of *Adam:* sith our erected wit maketh vs know what perfection is, and yet our infected will keepeth vs from reaching vnto it.[1]

At best, the poet may create a pattern of excellence. Or he

1. "An Apologie for Poetrie," in *Elizabethan Critical Essays*, ed. G. Gregory Smith (Oxford, 1904), 1 : 157.

may, as the doubting Theseus has it, be one with the lunatic
and the lover, creating out of nothing—nothing:

> The poet's eye, in a fine frenzy rolling,
> Doth glance from heaven to earth, from earth to heaven;
> And as imagination bodies forth
> The forms of things unknown, the poet's pen
> Turns them to shapes, and gives to airy nothing
> A local habitation and a name.
>
> [*Midsummer Night's Dream*, V.i.12]

Or he may do worse. Plato therefore, of whom Sidney was
trying to make an ally, had banished poets from his ideal
state because he feared the poet's power to create the moral
equivalent of "nothing," falsehood. Not, of course, that every
fiction is false: Plato himself, like Jesus, was a master of the
parable; but behind the allowable fable must stand the essential truth it figures forth. The danger comes in the lying
fable; and the same quality of delight through which the
truthful poet (be his truth Platonic or Christian) ministers
"a medicine of Cherries," may make us suck up poison un-
awares.

There is abundant evidence that Shakespeare felt this
danger. Most obvious is the fact that a great many of his references to his own profession associate it with evil. The stage-
player (and especially the tragedian) tends to merge with the
figure of the Machiavellian. But we ought not to make too
much of this fact. Such references tend toward the merely
conventional, and tend also to be too general, associating evil
with hypocrisy, and hypocrisy (in turn) with all sorts of
vaguely histrionic pursuits. The future Richard III's statement
of intent, in *3 Henry VI*, is a good example of what I mean,
for here the villian's association with the art of the stage is
almost lost in a busy catalog of deceivers:

> Why, I can smile, and murder whiles I smile,
> And cry 'Content!' to that which grieves my heart,
> And wet my cheeks with artificial tears,

And frame my face to all occasions.
I'll drown more sailors than the mermaid shall;
I'll slay more gazers than the basilisk;
I'll play the orator as well as Nestor,
Deceive more slily than Ulysses could,
And, like a Sinon, take another Troy.
I can add colours to the chameleon,
Change shapes with Proteus for advantages,
And set the murderous Machiavel to school.
Can I do this, and cannot get a crown?
Tut, were it further off, I'll pluck it down.
[III.ii.182]

We cannot, of course, entirely dismiss the epithets which suggest an affinity between the art of the stage and the artful villain; but we cannot assume, either, that they give us any great insight into Shakespeare's attitude toward his own art of words and gesture. For one thing, over-much attention to such epithets would lead to the conclusion (not quite absurd but certainly simplistic) that Shakespeare despised his art. And, for another, there are better, more interesting places to look.

I hope I have already suggested some such places. In *Titus Andronicus,* for instance, I looked at the art of rhetoric and the question it raised of the relationship between man's need for expression and the only partial efficacy of words for fulfilling that need. In discussing *Hamlet* I made much ado of plays and playing within the play, and (not to draw it any finer) found that a play is a complex thing, both for good and for ill. In a more general way still, the discussion of *Troilus and Cressida* tried to reveal Shakespeare grappling with the question of form in art and (construing art as its metaphor) in life; again, we found a complex attitude, predominantly pessimistic but (because the play is successful as a play) not entirely so. In turning now to *Othello,* and then to *Macbeth,* I intend to organize the discussion around the most fundamental aspect of Shakespeare's art, the matter (to invoke

Wordsworth) of "Imagination—here the Power so called /
Through sad incompetence of human speech." I will be interested, that is, in the unique freedom Sidney grants the poet
in ranging within the zodiac of his own wit—or the folly, as
Theseus has it, in bodying forth the forms of things unknown.

And I begin with an observation about Iago so widely
known that only its rightness keeps it from being an embarrassment to me. It comes in a passage by A. C. Bradley, in
which he takes up a suggestion of Hazlitt's:

> But Iago, finally, is not simply a man of action; he is
> an artist. His action is a plot, the intricate plot of a drama,
> and in the conception and execution of it he experiences
> the tension and the joy of artistic creation "He is," says
> Hazlitt, "an amateur of tragedy in real life. . . ." [2]

A slight reformulation may be desirable; we may want
to insist that Iago is not an amateur of anything "in real life":
at best he is an amateur of tragedy within a tragedy, a creation
masquerading as a creator. But the Bradley-Hazlitt perception
of Iago as independent creator is not merely the product of a
worn-out critical mode. Of course Iago remains Shakespeare's
creature, but the illusion of reality is all to the point. Shakespeare's play, a fictive world, becomes for our purposes primary
reality; and Iago's way (which leads Bradley to call him an artist)
is to interpolate into that primary reality another "world," a
fiction-within-a-fiction. It is as if Shakespeare had admitted
into the zodiac of his wit a diabolical adversary. The outcome,
ultimately, cannot be in question, but the struggle is none the
less important for that. Two worlds, using (as we shall see)
languages that are virtually foreign to each other, battle for
predominance in *Othello,* and much of the play's dramatic
tension is generated as we wait in suspense for the necessary
but still mysterious outcome.

The objectivity of the dramatic mode, with its consequent
inevitable ambiguity, gives Iago the chance to impose his fic-

2. *Shakespearean Tragedy* (London, 1904), pp. 230–31.

tion upon the reality of the play. Othello and Desdemona are part of that "reality"; but, as we see repeatedly in Shakespeare, the distance between language and "reality," word and world, can be a source of menace—and the reality of Othello and Desdemona is one that taxes and exhausts the resources of language. They are opposites timely in their timelessness: black and white, old and young, barbarian and Venetian. How shall one speak of them? Here, at one extreme, may be that perfect union of opposites which should make us cry, " 'How true a twain / Seemeth this concordant one!'," the marriage that confounds reason by showing "division grow together" ("The Phoenix and the Turtle," ll. 45, 42).[3] But here, too, may be a violation of nature so profound that only the most disgusting of bestial imagery could describe it, "an old black ram . . . tupping [a] white ewe," a "beast with two backs" which will give to a "reverend signior" "coursers for cousins and gennets for germans."

For us, as audience, the possibilities are of course not that wide: the latter interpretation is Iago's, and we know—even without having yet encountered Othello himself—that it comes from a man with a grudge, is a put-up job, and cannot be believed. But if it is true that not every interpretation is equally valid, we may also feel, when we have actually met Othello and Desdemona—and heard them speak in tones uniquely theirs, the mark of their individuality—that no single interpretive guess will be wholly adequate. Always they will elude our attempts to formulate them in words. We can know them, but how shall we speak of them as they are?

The difficulty begins as soon as we hear Othello speak. His words have ascertainable meanings, but are they the words of a self-dramatizing weakling overcompensating for a lack of real social assurance, or are they the warm and expansive words of a generous-souled warrior? [4]

3. Cf. Bernard Spivack, *Shakespeare and the Allegory of Evil* (New York, 1958), pp. 422 ff.

4. Notable answers hostile to Othello have come from: T. S. Eliot, "Shakespeare and the Stoicism of Seneca," in *Selected Essays*, 2d rev. ed.

Let him do this spite.
My services which I have done the signiory
Shall out-tongue his complaints. 'Tis yet to know—
Which, when I know that boasting is an honour,
I shall promulgate—I fetch my life and being
From men of royal seige; and my demerits
May speak unbonneted to as proud a fortune
As this that I have reach'd.

[I.ii.17]

Desdemona, whose fate is sufficient to secure her from harsh criticism, is generally let go unscathed; but she too, as much as Othello, is finally unformulable. What, for instance, are we to make of this "round unvarnish'd tale" Othello delivers about his "whole course of love"? Is the Desdemona of that tale "A maiden never bold, / Of spirit so still and quiet that her motion / Blush'd at herself" (I.iii.94), or indeed a "super-subtle Venetian" in her response to Othello's tale of wonder?

My story being done,
She gave me for my pains a world of sighs;
She swore, in faith, 'twas strange, 'twas passing strange;
'Twas pitiful, 'twas wondrous pitiful.
She wish'd she had not heard it; yet she wish'd
That heaven had made her such a man. She thank'd me;
And bade me, if I had a friend that lov'd her,
I should but teach him how to tell my story,
And that would woo her. Upon this hint I spake;
She lov'd me for the dangers I had pass'd;
And I lov'd her that she did pity them.

[I.iii.158]

(London, 1934), pp. 126–40; F. R. Leavis, *The Common Pursuit* (London, 1952), pp. 136–59; D. A. Traversi, *An Approach to Shakespeare*, 2d rev. ed. (Garden City, N.Y., 1956), pp. 128–50. For the defense: Helen Gardner, *The Noble Moor* (London, 1955); John Bayley, *The Characters of Love* (London, 1960), pp. 125–202; John Holloway, *The Story of the Night* (Lincoln, Neb., 1961), pp. 155–65.

The matter is not one of pure relativity: it would indeed take an Iago to find in Desdemona's little stratagems—in the very transparency of them—anything particularly culpable. Desdemona's wiles may make her something less than perfect, but they also make her "real." And built into that quality of realism is the inevitable residue of ambiguity which makes words such poor instruments for speaking of Desdemona as she is, with nothing extenuated and nought set down in malice. Shortly we shall see how Iago, when he sets to work on Othello, need only recur to this "round unvarnish'd tale": there is little for him to invent, only a new interpretation—a new verbal approximation of the experienced reality—to provide.

The inadequacy of language as a substitute for complex reality is a problem that first becomes apparent in the case of the outraged father, Brabantio. Brabantio has had his secure sleep interrupted by the voices of Iago and Roderigo—loud, rude, obscene—which pierce the Venetian quiet,

> with like timorous accent and dire yell
> As when, by night or negligence, the fire
> Is spied in populous cities.
> [I.i.76]

They bring extraordinary news: the young and beautiful daughter of the senator has eloped with an aging black man, a professional soldier with an adventurer's past. The principals to this startling event have come before the Senate (I.iii) to make charges and give explanations. And the Senate, a body engaged in separating true intelligence from false, deciding which of the enemy's moves is merely "a pageant / To keep us in false gaze," and which represents his true intents, has handled the domestic danger with accustomed ease. Othello and Desdemona are vindicated, and Brabantio must abide by the decision.

But Brabantio need not like it, and in his dissatisfaction he refers specifically to a failure of language. The Duke has offered Brabantio a series of good moral *sententiae* intended to make his bitter experience palatable:

When remedies are past, the griefs are ended
By seeing the worst, which late on hopes depended.
To mourn a mischief that is past and gone
Is the next way to draw new mischief on.
What cannot be preserv'd when fortune takes,
Patience her injury a mockery makes.
The robb'd that smiles steals something from the thief;
He robs himself that spends a bootless grief.

[I.iii.202]

Brabantio, however, rejects this insipid fare, substituting for it
his own mocking version of the Duke's sentences:

So let the Turk of Cyprus us beguile:
We lose it not so long as we can smile.
He bears the sentence well that nothing bears
But the free comfort which from thence he hears;
But he bears both the sentence and the sorrow
That to pay grief must of poor patience borrow.
These sentences, to sugar or to gall,
Being strong on both sides, are equivocal.
But words are words: I never yet did hear
That the bruis'd heart was pierced through the ear.

[210]

In Brabantio's bitter mockery is recognition of the gulf between words and the situation they are meant to describe and
deal with. The Duke's words are "equivocal" because the key
to any speech-event must be the interpretation made by the
recipient; and in this case Brabantio decodes the message according to values and presuppositions different from the
sender's. The Senate may enforce a show of unanimity, a
pretense that this world is univocal in its symbolic structure;
but Brabantio's insistence that, in face of his actual grief all
words are equivocal, reveals a weakness in that structure.

Even the style of the Duke's consoling speech is revealing.
In a play so rich in the poetry both of love and hate, the
Duke's sentences stand out as a moment when Shakespeare
seems to nod. And the jigging badness of the Duke's verse is

made especially egregious by the poetic magnificence that has just preceded it. For we have just heard Othello's "round unvarnish'd tale," which includes "moving accidents by flood and field" and amazing encounters with "the Cannibals that each other eat, / The Anthropophagi, and men whose heads / Do grow beneath their shoulders"—as well as the equally astonishing account of Desdemona's response to that history. It is a speech that elicits from the Duke one line of perfect literary criticism: "I think this tale would win my daughter too." But when in his sententious speech the Duke proceeds (as in effect he does) to offer an interpretation of Othello's tale for Brabantio's benefit, we leave the sublime for the almost ridiculous. Brabantio's mocking reply, however, shows that Shakespeare has only seemed to nod. The disparity between Othello's verse and the Duke's is a purposeful demonstration of the distance between the vibrant complexity of immediate experience and even the best intentioned efforts to reformulate that experience. That the Duke's consolatory speech should be inadequate to the point of travesty is entirely appropriate.

"I never yet did hear / That the bruis'd heart was pierced through the ear"—Brabantio's final thrust reminds us that language can offer both hope and threat. There has been no essential communication between Brabantio and the Duke because their words do not refer to each other's "reality." Brabantio's parodic reply warns, implicitly, that despite an apparently shared language, each man remains locked in a private reality from which (like the Senate on watch for the treacherous Turk) he can only make guesses about the reality without.

And it is this isolation that Iago will exploit. Again, it is with Brabantio that we get our first insight into Iago's way. Brabantio's shocked reply to the outrageous voices of Iago and Roderigo had been, at first, the confident assertion, "This is Venice; / My house is not a grange" (I.i.106). But Iago quickly succeeds here, as he will do later, in using words to interpolate into that secure world another "reality" which is indeed a wild place filled with grotesque and threatening forms of bestial life. The human beings we call Othello and

Desdemona become, in Iago's descriptions, ugly beasts caught
in postures out of a nightmare *Metamorphoses;* the Brabantio
who comes before the Senate is a man whose Venice has become that grange he previously thought it could not be.
Brabantio's world, once he has been awakened from his placid
sleep, is a world summoned into being by Iago's words, and
now the words of that other Venice cannot be understood by
him. Brabantio's wild city is not the real Venice; it is a mere
fiction, but made by Iago a potent, destructive force. As we
watch Iago working upon Brabantio, we see the creation of
that false world which will vie throughout the play with
Shakespeare's truth.

On the basis of Iago's initial success, the plan he begins to
formulate for Othello's ruin must seem particularly auspicious:
"After some time to abuse Othello's ear" (I.iii.389). Iago's
words, which exploit the equivocation at the heart of Venice's
order, have already made the city a "grange" surrounded by
prodigies of nature and sexual appetite. Now, again with
words ("I'll pour this pestilence into his ear" [II.iii.345]), Iago
will draw Othello into that bestial world, will put into his
mouth the uncouth words of that world, and will make him
deaf to the voices of the civil city.

With the work of the Senate concluded—Othello is dis-
patched to Cyprus and Desdemona allowed to accompany him
—the plot quickly moves forward. Or, rather, the *plots,* for
there is both Shakespeare's plot and Iago's, the latter a "plot"
which proceeds according to that secondary "reality" Iago
interpolates upon the primary one. Verbal and dramatic
ironies become the measure of the distance between those
two plots, and words themselves become charged with menace.
Othello introduces Iago to the Duke with words that will
reverberate throughout the play:

> So please your grace, my ancient;
> A man he is of honesty and trust.
> To his conveyance I assign my wife. . . .
>   [I.iii.283]

Along with this first appearance of the "honest" Iago, the coming danger is emphasized with a pun: "conveyance," along with the meaning intended by Othello, also has the meaning of trickery or even outright theft. To Brabantio's warning, "Look to her, Moor, if thou hast eyes to see: / She has deceiv'd her father, and may thee," Othello swears, "My life upon her faith! —Honest Iago, / My Desdemona must I leave to thee" (294).

Iago's stage is the island of Cyprus, to which the action moves at the opening of Act II. Like Venice, Cyprus is a place where men are engaged in making guesses about a reality that resists interpretation. The first line of Act II is a question, "What from the cape can you discern at sea?" and as news arrives of the Turkish fleet's destruction, the men of Cyprus continue to watch the mysterious sea, "even till [they] make the main and th' aerial blue / An indistinct regard" (39), for the arrival of the passengers from Venice. Cassio is first to arrive; his answer to Montano's question—"But, good lieutenant, is your general wiv'd"?—is another reminder of the inadequacy of words in resolving our questions about reality, for his only answer is an assertion of the impossibility of describing Desdemona: she is one, he says, "that paragons description and wild fame; / One that excels the quirks of blazoning pens" (II.i.62).

Iago and Desdemona, with Roderigo doggedly in tow, come ashore next. And now, as all await news of Othello, it is Iago's turn to give us some insight into the worth of words. Specifically, it is the question of Emilia's *speaking* which calls forth Iago's animadversions upon women. Iago claims that Emilia bestows her tongue too liberally, although Desdemona protests (in a line that will become grimly ironic by Act V), "Alas, she has no speech!" (103). Iago shifts from the specific accusation to a general one, to an attempt to formulate women as a class—a process (and a style of verse) that may remind us of the Duke's attempt to move from Brabantio's particular grief to generalized moral reflection.

Like the Duke's *sententiae*, Iago's scurrilous generalizations are inadequate to the point of travesty. (His only remark that bears the ring of truth is the protest, "Nay, it is true, or else I am a Turk.") But it seems a harmless enough game, and so, to pass the anxious time of waiting, Desdemona urges Iago to persist. Iago's "Muse labours, and thus she is deliver'd" of a series of rhymed strictures upon the various types of women. They are, as Desdemona protests, "old fond paradoxes to make fools laugh i' th' alehouse," but that rough quality itself might give them some credence, especially among those who prefer the blunt speech of the alehouse to the scholar's hesitant respect for ambiguity: as Cassio puts it, "He speaks home, madam. You may relish him more in the soldier than in the scholar" (165).

It is a mere game with words Iago is playing, but Iago plays for keeps. And immediately following Cassio's defense of him, Iago shows a potentially more serious use he can make of his Muse's talents. As he watches Cassio pay innocent court to Desdemona, Iago speaks aside and reveals how easily he will be able to convert innocence into its opposite. Slander of a class changes to slander of an individual, and Iago's game becomes earnest indeed:

> He takes her by the palm. Ay, well said, whisper. With as little a web as this will I ensnare as great a fly as Cassio. Ay, smile upon her, do; I will gyve thee in thine own courtship. You say true; 'tis so, indeed. If such tricks as these strip you out of your lieutenantry, it had been better you had not kiss'd your three fingers so oft, which now again you are most apt to play the sir in. Very good; well kissed! and excellent courtesy! 'Tis so, indeed. Yet again your fingers to your lips? Would they were clyster-pipes for your sake! [II.i.166]

And with the latest of the pornographic word-pictures Iago is so adept at creating—and at making the gullible accept as objective reality—the trumpet is heard announcing Othello's arrival in Cyprus.

Iago's exposition of the plot he is setting in motion shows that creative delight which Hazlitt and Bradley noticed. His first act involves Cassio's disgrace:

If I can fasten but one cup upon him,
With that which he hath drunk to-night already,
He'll be as full of quarrel and offence
As my young mistress' dog. Now my sick fool Roderigo,
Whom love hath turn'd almost the wrong side outward,
To Desdemona hath to-night carous'd
Potations pottle deep; and he's to watch.
Three else of Cyprus—noble swelling spirits,
That hold their honours in a wary distance,
The very elements of this warlike isle—
Have I to-night fluster'd with flowing cups,
And they watch too. Now, 'mongst this flock of drunkards
Am I to put our Cassio in some action
That may offend the isle—but here they come.

[II.iii.44]

The setting is, appropriately, the citadel's court of guard. Appropriately, because this setting (like the Senate in Venice) is a visible sign of the state's order; it is a place from which to look abroad for the enemy Turk and to maintain the domestic calm of "a town of war, / Yet wild" (II.iii.205). The ritual of the place is as absolute as military ritual can be; but Iago turns that ritual into its opposite—a counter-ritual—a confused, drunken brawl in which general discipline gives way to individual antagonism. Othello's angry entrance into this scene of confusion shows how accurately Iago has hit his mark. So totally has he perverted the ritual of the guard that Othello must ask, "Are we turn'd Turks, and to ourselves do that / Which heaven hath forbid the Ottomites?" (II.iii.162). And Cassio, who in this counter-ritual has been forced to play a role so very different from his accustomed one, now finds himself speechless *in propria persona*: to Othello's question, "How comes it, Michael, you are thus forgot?" he can only reply, "I pray you, pardon me; I cannot speak" (II.iii.180).

Cassio's momentary aphasia (and his previous drunken speech, so unlike his ordinary manner) is exactly the sort of triumph at which Iago aims and which he will shortly achieve, even beyond his own expectation, with Othello. To Cassio, the culprit seems clearly and singly the wine; but with the sort of verbal irony typical of the play, he identifies that culprit by the same name Othello will later use to identify Iago: "O thou invisible spirit of wine, if thou hast no name to be known by, let us call thee devil!" (II.iii.274). Shortly, when we hear Othello ranting of goats and toads and monkeys, Cassio's remorseful self-accusation may seem to offer a model for the entire Iago-plot. "O God," Cassio moans, "that men should put an enemy in their mouths to steal away their brains! That we should with joy, pleasance, revel and applause, transform ourselves into beasts!" (280). The progress Cassio has gone neatly defines the progress Othello will also go: "To be now a sensible man, by and by a fool, and presently a beast! O strange!" (295).

Traditionally, the poet uses a fable to sugar-coat his pill of truth. But Iago, the imaginative diabolist, reverses the process, using truth to make Othello swallow his liquor of deceit. Thus, for instance, he truly cautions his victim,

> I perchance am vicious in my guess,
> As, to confess, it is my nature's plague
> To spy into abuses, and oft my jealousy
> Shapes faults that are not. . . .
>
> [III.iii.149]

and by taking one step backward moves forward two. Or, again, perfectly defining his inner core of mystery, he responds to Othello's "By heaven, I'll know thy thoughts," with "You cannot, if my heart were in your hand" (166). Othello may reassure himself that "she had eyes, and chose me" (193), but Iago need only describe the manner of Desdemona's choosing to convert it to harm:

> She did deceive her father, marrying you;
> And when she seem'd to shake and fear your looks,
> She lov'd them most.
>
> [III.iii.210]

From that true-enough reminder it is but a step to the hint,

> Why, go to then!
> She that, so young, could give out such a seeming,
> To seel her father's eyes up close as oak—
> He thought 'twas witchcraft. But I am much to blame. . . .
> [212]

The stages of Othello's intoxication are subtle: there will
always remain something of mystery, of "witchcraft," in Iago's
triumph.[5] And it is in large part Iago's apparent truth-telling
which creates that mystery. At his terrifying best, Iago does
not quite lie; he merely exploits the inherent distance between
word and world. But in saying that Iago's truth-telling is one
of his most diabolical aspects, I do not mean simply that the
devil can speak true: other personages do that as well. I mean
that Iago's truth-telling acts as a sort of black magic, taking
possession of the thing through manipulation of its symbol.
Iago's perverse redaction of Othello's "round unvarnish'd tale"
of love, in which Desdemona's innocently feminine actions become politic dissemblings, does not merely sully the event and
its memory: the repetition of the words seems actually to take
it over, to capture it; and as the memory of the courtship
passes (through the medium of Iago's words) from Othello's to
Iago's sphere of influence, a part of Othello seems to go into
Iago's power as well. "I am bound to thee forever," says
Othello after Iago's reminders—and this is the bond which
separates him from the world of primary reality and traps him
in the fantasy imagined into existence by Iago.

At the end of the temptation scene, Iago and Othello kneel
together and reaffirm that bond through a formal rite. Othello,
now in Iago's power and (as we shall see) understanding only
the fantastic Iago-semantic, declares:

> Now, by yond marble heaven,
> In the due reverence of a sacred vow
> I here engage my words.
> [III.iii.464]

5. On the centrality of the ambiguous word *witchcraft*, see Robert
Heilman's indispensable study, *Magic in the Web* (Lexington, Ky., 1956),
especially p. 225.

At this instant the kneeling Othello belongs to the same myth as the Faustus who writes his name in blood for Mephistopheles. Like Faustus, Othello will now consistently misinterpret the world, and the words, around him. He will live in that hell uncircumscribed of which, in this play, Iago is chief citizen. And while others will see Othello and hear him speak, there will be no real communication with him from the world he has left. Now, as Iago says in an interestingly reversed formulation, "I am your own for ever" (III.iii.end).

From the time of Othello's reentry in Act III, scene 3 (marked for us by Iago's ironic observation—which will remind us of Brabantio's "awakening"—that nothing now can medicine Othello "to that sweet sleep" [336] he had known yesterday), Othello lives in the false world imagined into being by Iago and his latest too-willing accomplice. Now the impossible world of Desdemona's "stol'n hours of lust," populated (as it was, also, for Brabantio) by horrible forms of bestial life, is the world Othello takes for the real world. The ceremony he and Iago perform in engaging their words is the first in a series of counter-rituals which replace the rituals of the world Othello has left and define the new one he has entered. (The series is completed with Desdemona's murder, when Othello acts out the counter-ritual—a parody of justice complete with trial and execution—to replace the marriage that defined the old world.)

But while Othello acts and speaks on the premises of the new Iago-world, the other characters continue to act and speak in the manner of the old. And because each world has its own entirely different history and consequent set of values, the language of each (although phonetically identical) is unintelligible to the other. There is speech between the inhabitants of the two worlds, but no communication; as Desdemona says to Othello, "I understand a fury in your words, / But not the words" (IV.ii.32; not in Folio). Thus two separate and contradictory plots are played out on the same stage; characters, as well as audience, watch the unsettling spectacle of a man living in a dream.

Othello himself defines for us the distance between the Iago-world and that other world in which Desdemona, having eyes, chose him; I refer to his speech of farewell to that world:

> O, now for ever
> Farewell the tranquil mind! farewell content!
> Farewell the plumed troops, and the big wars
> That makes ambition virtue! O, farewell!
> Farewell the neighing steed and the shrill trump,
> The spirit-stirring drum, th' ear-piercing fife,
> The royal banner, and all quality,
> Pride, pomp, and circumstance, of glorious war!
> And O ye mortal engines whose rude throats
> Th' immortal Jove's dread clamours counterfeit,
> Farewell! Othello's occupation's gone.
> [III.iii.351]

The speech is not an over-reaction, or an example of Othello "cheering himself up." Desdemona's integrity has been the guarantor of Othello's integrity, of his sense of himself as Othello; in her he has "garner'd up [his] heart," and in her "must live or bear no life." Now he finds himself discarded from "The fountain from which [his] current runs," a fountain which has become (in words that clearly suggest the source of the pollution) "A cistern for foul toads / To knot and gender in" (IV.ii.58–63).

Thus with Desdemona's loss, Othello feels the loss of all the warrants, the points of security, the values, which have informed his life. He had called her, improbably but rightly, his "fair warrior" (II.i.180); and Desdemona too, even after the estrangement, calls herself an "unhandsome warrior" (III.iv.152): the paradox that makes of a gentle girl a "warrior" is like the paradox of the marriage itself, the union of opposites into a more perfect whole. Desdemona is, with very little exaggeration, Othello's occupation, and his farewell to her quite properly includes his farewell to the world of battle which she (woman and warrior) has warranted.

We have already seen in this study a man in a position

similar to Othello's, and the experience of each casts light upon the other: Troilus, too, found his whole world subverted by the infidelity of the person who gave it meaning. Both men suffer—Troilus in the knotty intellectual language of his play, Othello in the passionate language of his—the shattering of an entire symbolic system. With Troilus's "This is, and is not, Cressid," we may compare Othello's "I think my wife be honest, and think she is not" (III.iii.388). In both cases, the doubt about the "rule in unity" calls into question not only the identity of the other person, but the identity of the questioner himself. "When one's real life is in one's loyalties and actions," Northrop Frye writes, "all that the isolated mind can attain is an awareness of absurdity. . . . Once withdrawn from the course of action which holds us within society, chaos is come again." [6]

We have seen Troilus try to reason his way (through paradox, and quite unsuccessfully) out of that chaos. Othello grasps at a more direct means of restoring some comprehensible system: "Villain," he demands of Iago, "be sure thou prove my love a whore" (III.iii. 363). His demands and pleas—"give me the ocular proof," "make me to see't," "Would I were satisfied!"—are the cries of a man who finds himself banished from society's guarded city to the unformed wilderness of the self. Desdemona has been, by his own assertion, his bulwark against chaos; now the warrior who once faced "anters vast and deserts wild" in the pursuance of an ideal and an occupation, finds the world without Desdemona a desert too horrible to contemplate, and turns, with terrifying haste, to Iago for relief.

And Iago is waiting to welcome him to a world where doubt is resolved. But—and this is what gives the peculiar horror to Othello's situation—the relief is quite the reverse of a return from solipsism; it is, rather, a bond with solipsism and an estrangement from waking reality. Othello's demand for "ocular proof" is all the more terrifying in that what he demands

6. *Fools of Time* (Toronto, 1967), p. 101. There is an interesting comparison of Troilus and Othello in Norman Rabkin's *Shakespeare and the Common Understanding* (New York, 1967), pp. 57–58.

to see is, literally, nothing, a falsehood. And Iago has the audacity to adduce as such a proof a mere dream—or rather, the dream of a dream, for his tale of how Cassio muttered in his sleep about an affair with Desdemona is just another obscene creation ex nihilo. Yet Othello, in his desperation, finds " 'Tis a shrewd doubt, though it be but a dream" (II.iii. 433). Cassio's dream, like the rest of Iago's plot, is unreal, but into that double unreality—a fictive dream—Othello madly rushes.

His situation finds emblematic enactment in Act IV, scene 1, where Othello watches, but does not hear or understand, Iago's carefully stage-managed conversation with Cassio. "Do but encave yourself," Iago directs him (using a particularly suitable verb),

> And mark the fleers, the gibes, and notable scorns,
> That dwell in every region of his face;
> For I will make him tell the tale anew—
> Where, how, how oft, how long ago, and when,
> He hath, and is again to cope your wife.
> I say, but mark his gesture.
>   [IV.i.81]

But Cassio's gestures come from a world Othello has already left. The play in which Cassio is still an actor is now all inexplicable dumb-show to Othello, and the words Othello finds to match the gestures are words drawn from the Iago-plot. Two different semantics share the stage, each reflecting the mutually exclusive "truth" of its own world. And from now on in the play, incomprehension of this sort will mark the succeeding encounters between Othello and the other characters. Lodovico, for instance, arrives with letters from the Senate; Othello, unable to contain himself, mutters threats and curses at Desdemona which the others are unable to interpret:

> *Des.* What, is he angry?
> *Lod.*   May be the letter mov'd him.
>   [IV.i.231]

Othello strikes Desdemona; he babbles, half about the Venetian business, half about his wife; finally he flings offstage with
the cry (drawn from the Iago-language), "Goats and monkeys!" (260). And Lodovico is left to express his astonishment
at the terrible charade he has seen:

> Is this the noble Moor whom our full Senate
> Call all in all sufficient? Is this the nature
> Whom passion could not shake, whose solid virtue
> The shot of accident nor the dart of chance
> Could neither graze nor pierce?
>
> [IV.i.261]

Iago's comment is the laconic, "He is much chang'd."

In the next encounter between Othello and Desdemona
(IV.ii), we see the logic of the Iago-plot (in which Desdemona
plays a role similar to that filled in the primary play by the
courtesan Bianca) working itself out in the other "plot" as a
dreadful illogic. Emilia becomes the bawd to whore Desdemona, and Othello, speaking as if he were a customer in a
brothel, bids, "Some of your function, mistress: / Leave pro-
creants alone, and shut the door" (27). Desdemona, who understands the fury but not the words, protests, to Othello's question, "Why, what art thou?", "Your wife, my lord, your true
and loyal wife." But it is too late for that simple communication to be understood. Now it can only double-damn her to
swear that she is honest; and if she persists in denying that
she is a whore, Othello must acknowledge his mistake by
saying,

> I cry you mercy, then.
> I took you for that cunning whore of Venice
> That married with Othello.
>
> [89]

And, like Troilus denying the "rule in unity," Othello dismisses her as the wrong person. The bawd Emilia is given
money for her pains, and Othello leaves the stage, not to re-
appear until he comes to play out the last act of the Iago-plot.

That plot (as Hazlitt suggested) is a tragedy-within-a-tragedy. The situation may be compared structurally with the one we found in *Julius Caesar*. Although there is on the surface little similarity between Othello and the stoic Brutus, both men, in their dramatic careers, make a similar mistake: both cast the wrong person in the role of tragic victim. And as Brutus had pleaded, "Let's be sacrificers, but not butchers, Caius," so Othello urges (though with less conviction now) the distinction between gratuitous murder and necessary sacrifice:

> O perjur'd woman! thou dost stone my heart,
> And mak'st me call what I intend to do
> A murder, which I thought a sacrifice.
> [V.ii.66]

This murder which Othello has conceived as sacrifice is the culminating ritual in the Iago-tragedy; but in the play *Othello* it is chaos come again. The confusion between the two words *murder* and *sacrifice* is the final terminological confusion, attesting to the equivocal nature of the "reality" beyond language, in a play which has moved from verbal ironies to a split between rival semantic systems. Desdemona's death is the last action of the Iago-plot and the final statement of the Iago-language. But now another language will be heard and another ritual enacted.

For although Iago may precipitate his drama-within-the-drama, still he must be subject finally to the single destiny of Shakespeare's plot. And if we see that formal necessity in light of Philip Sidney's analogy between the poetic maker and "the heuenly Maker of that maker," we may find interesting implications in it. The moralist's charge against the poet is that he lies—and Shakespeare has admitted into his poetic universe a secondary world compounded entirely of lies. Sidney's analogy turns the formal requirement that only Shakespeare's "truth" can prevail, into a structural metaphor for matters moral and even theological. The good in this play (Desdemona and the waking world) is *real*, but evil (Iago's hallucinatory world) is *unreal*. In some traditional theologies, evil has power only when men turn away from the real (the good) and *imagine* that evil is real.[7]

Shakespeare's play is analogous to the Word of God (it is truth incarnate), but the words of the Iago-plot are the words of the perverted imagination, masquerading as truth and potent only until revealed (by a cleared perception) in their essential unreality. If, as Bradley writes, "Nowhere else in Shakespeare do we hold our breath in such anxiety and for so long a time as in the later Acts of *Othello*," [8] much of that tension results from our expectation of the unmasking. Because Othello's crime is also an error of the imagination (Bradley calls it "a hideous blunder"), the audience must feel (however decorously it behaves) like children at a pantomime or villagers at a pageant: we feel like crying out, "Look behind you! It's the devil!"

And, typically, Shakespeare takes account of this feeling in the audience and makes it part of his dramatic material. No sooner is Othello's dreadful counter-ritual enacted than Emilia's cry is heard from within the chamber, "O, good my lord, I'd speak a word with you!" (V.ii.93). Othello has become deaf to the language of ordinary life and tragically isolated from the world around him; now, with a vehemence and "iterance" sufficient to overcome the horror of that deafness, the world thrusts itself back at Othello, demanding to be heard. By my conservative estimate, the word *speak* and related words such as *tell, relate,* and *say* are repeated at least thirty-six times in the approximately 280 lines left in the play. Othello knows that Emilia will "speak of Cassio's death," and fears that "she'll sure speak to my wife" (V.ii.95, 99). He hesitates while Emilia calls again, "I do beseech you that I may speak with you" (104). The language of reality demands to be heard; the simple unheroic voice of Emilia speaks (as Bradley observes) for the audience, expressing our horror at the murder (and the mistake) and, most importantly, opening the ears of Othello.

---

7. See the account of the theology of Athanasius by Jaroslav Pelikan, *The Light of the World* (New York, 1962).

8. *Shakespearean Tragedy*, p. 180.

The communication comes slowly, with difficulty. Othello names Emilia's husband as the source of the horror, and four times Emilia repeats the incomprehensible message, "My husband?" Iago now appears on stage with the others, and to Emilia's assertion, "You told a lie—an odious damned lie," he bids her, "Go to, charm your tongue." (We recall now the irony of Desdemona's defense of Emilia: "Alas, she hath no tongue.") But the language of reality, the language of the play's dramatic destiny, cannot be stilled: "I will not charm my tongue; I am bound to speak" (187), and "Good gentlemen, let me have leave to speak" (198), and

> 'Twill out, 'twill out. I, peace!
> No, I will speak as liberal as the north.
> Let heaven and men and devils, let them all,
> All, all, cry shame against me, yet I'll speak.
> [V.ii.222]

Emilia's iterated words make their attack upon the unreality of evil, exorcising that fantastic Iago-language which had cast its spell over Othello. Her final words bear the simple message of truth, the message the audience has wanted to shout: "Moor, she was chaste; she lov'd thee, cruel Moor" (252). But evil, whose essence is to be false and which cannot speak truth however much men's ignorance may for a time construe its words for truth; evil, in the person of Iago, must end in the silence that is its only truthful expression. Othello demands of "that demi-devil / Why he hath thus ensnar'd my soul and body," and Iago's only reply is the stubborn, empty, and necessary, "Demand me nothing. What you know, you know. / From this time forth I never will speak word" (304, 306).

I have said that the language of reality bursts through the final scene exorcising the false language of evil, but we have not yet seen the full extent of that revelation. For it is not only Emilia who demands to speak and be heard; Desdemona herself, as if from death, cries out her message, "O, falsely, falsely murder'd" (120). Desdemona had been, for Othello, the symbol and warrant of reality; when he turned from her he bade farewell to his "occupation" and made his bond with the Iago-world. But even murdered, she will make herself heard, interposing against the falseness of evil. And how gently ironic, for all the horror, Shakespeare makes this nearly miraculous speech! For Desdemona's last words, the very words of truth, contain a lie: Emilia asks, "O, who hath done this deed?" and Desdemona replies, "Nobody. I myself. Farewell. / Commend me to my kind lord. O, farewell!" (126). But, of course, it is a lie that could never deceive; and we may be reminded by Desdemona's last words of those little stratagems she had used when Othello first wooed her—of, for instance, the transparent ploy, "if I had a friend that lov'd her"—and notice that all the "lies" of goodness are fictions that speak a plain truth. Thus goodness will manifest itself, if only men will hear clearly and interpret aright.

But there is always the need to interpret. It can be a difficult task, and the price of failure may be the imposition of evil upon the world. As the imperative to speak echoes throughout the closing scene, so too the need to interpret, to understand what is spoken, becomes an explicit concern. Othello, released from his bondage to Iago, demands to speak a last time: "Soft you, a word or two before you go." Once more, as at the beginning of the play, he speaks with "the *Othello* music" [9] and not the hectic language of jealousy and hate. But the speech is only a beginning: it too must be heard and interpreted. Lodovico, the messenger from Venice, had asked Othello, "What shall be said to thee?" (296), and now Othello himself recurs to the difficulty in finding the proper words to match elusive reality:

> I pray you, in your letters,
> When you shall these unlucky deeds relate,
> Speak of me as I am; nothing extenuate,
> Nor set down aught in malice.
>
> [343]

9. The phrase is from G. Wilson Knight's essay of that title in *The Wheel of Fire*, 4th ed. revised and enlarged (London, 1949).

To our proxy, Lodovico, there comes (as there came to Horatio) the task of reporting the words and gestures he has witnessed. There is some irony in the fact that the very speech in which Othello lays that charge upon Lodovico—and through him, on us—has been used (by T. S. Eliot, for instance) as evidence for demeaning Othello's character. But such is the peril to which we are exposed, because (as Mr. Eliot's Sweeney knew) we've gotta use words when we talk to men. There is the deed, the verifiable act—our world, or that of a play like *Othello*—and there are the words by which its witnesses try to describe and interpret its meaning. Shakespeare has defined the risks: Lodovico "will straight abroad; and to the state / This heavy act with heavy heart relate"—but Othello knows that the messenger may not be able to speak of him as he is; and Iago remains silent, unexplained.

6

Macbeth

Macbeth is a play about evil, which is to say (with only a slight bow toward rhetorical neatness) that it is a play about *nothing* —for "evil is nothing, since God, who can do all things, cannot do evil" (Boethius, *Consolation*, Book III, Prose 12).[1] And with the play's very first line, the embodiment of nothingness enters upon the stage, raising immediately the ontological paradoxes inherent in the very idea of *nothing*.

True, the Weird Sisters are there; in some sense they must exist; and yet Banquo's question, "Are ye fantastical, or that indeed / Which outwardly ye show?" (I.iii.53) is hardly idle. They are the bubbles of the earth and they disappear into thin air; Banquo must wonder if he has not eaten some "insane root / That takes the reason prisoner" (84). Where the Weird Sisters preside, "nothing is but what is not"—yet how can we even say that "nothing *is*," since if it *is* then it is not *nothing*? (Yet if it is not something how could we truly conceive it?) The very notion of nothing "resist[s] domestication within the mind: [it is] also psychologically destructive, threatening the familiar boundaries of human experience and of intellectual efforts to get the better of that recalcitrant experience."[2] The absence, the sheer negative, which is evil, is corporealized from the first instant of *Macbeth;* and everything about it demands an extraordinary effort at interpretation.

---

1. *The Consolation of Philosophy*, trans. Richard Green (Indianapolis and New York, 1962), p. 72.

2. Rosalie Colie, *Paradoxia Epidemica* (Princeton, N.J., 1966), p. 222; see pp. 220–51 passim for an excellent discussion (to which I am indebted) of the "problem of nothing."

The Weird Sisters' rapid tetrameter verse hardly invites us to pause and ponder, but it will be necessary to do so nonetheless. For one thing, it will be clear that the problems they raise are related to problems we have encountered elsewhere. Despite its curious rhetoric, the paradox "Fair is foul, and foul is fair" is related to the sort of statement we have seen marking a tragedy's point of crisis; *Macbeth* is unique chiefly in the rapidity with which that point is reached. "Fair is foul, and foul is fair" reminds us of Troilus's recognition that the "rule in unity" has been destroyed, since "This is, and is not, Cressid." And it reminds us of the similar point in *Othello* where Desdemona also both is and is not Desdemona. And it reminds us of so many of the confusions in Hamlet's world, where funerals are marriages and where Claudius is Hamlet's mother, since "father and mother is man and wife, man and wife is one flesh, and so, my mother."

In each case, a perplexing gap is revealed between the literal meanings of words and the reality they can no longer describe in any terms except those of paradox or conundrum. Furthermore, the irruption of unreality onto the scene (which brings with it, as we shall see, its fantastic language of inversions) reminds us of the peculiar horror of Othello's situation: Othello, like Macbeth, accepts the unreality of evil in place of the normal reality of good; and both men are consequently plunged into a world of nightmare and hallucination, the most terrible aspect of which is its separation from the waking world around them.

But, of course, if it is true that the essential unreality of evil—the state in which "nothing is but what is not"—is its most terrible aspect, it is also its ultimate weakness. (Thus Boethius is consoled by Philosophy: "if our conclusion that evil is nothing still stands, it is clear that the wicked can do nothing since they can do only evil" [Book IV, Prose 2].[3] Evil exposed must, like Iago, remain silent and, in silence, reveal its insubstantiality. So in *Macbeth*, from the very beginning, we may notice that the potentially reason-destroying rhetoric

3. *Consolation of Philosophy*, p. 80.

*the either/or
does not admit
absurdity :*

of the Weird Sisters tends to be only *apparently* paradoxical: the riddles they pose, which at first glance seem to attest to a loss of universal cohesion (the "rule in unity"), are in fact capable of solution or will actually dissolve into "nothing" upon examination.

The Weird Sisters use a trick that would hardly have been news for the Delphic Oracle: through slight dislocations of normal grammatical or logical relationships, they make simple, even banal, statements sound as difficult as possible. That first portentous question, for instance, "When shall we three meet again? / In thunder, lightning, or in rain?" turns out to be more a phatic than a fatidic utterance when once we reflect that, in all probability, they will have to meet in thunder, lightning, *and* in rain. Similarly, the answer, "When the battle's lost and won," sounds, at first, deeply paradoxical; but the paradox is immediately unraveled, the implicit riddle solved, when we realize that every battle is both lost and won: the Weird Sisters, unlike a mortal audience, are simply not engaged on any particular side.

True, the riddle has still a further dimension, for there is a sense in which Macbeth's temporary victory—the satisfaction of his desires—will prove to be his ultimate loss: but, again, it is a comprehensible statement which leaves the "rule in unity" unimpaired. The possibility of real inversions are contained in the Weird Sisters' rhetoric, inversions that would prove the triumph of disorder, unreality, and evil over their opposites; but with each such possibility there coexists the possibility that the inversions are merely apparent and that a reasonable order, the order of normal good, remains only partially and temporarily obscured.

These first two instances of fiendish paltering prepare us for that curious statement, "Fair is foul, and foul is fair." Again, it is a statement with a "double sense," one of which is paradoxical and extraordinary, another simple and reasonable. As a metaphysical statement, "Fair is foul, and foul is fair," carries us beyond the normal limits of logical thought: if the values "fair" and "foul" have really been reversed, and the

reversals

things to which the words refer have really lost their identities, then the only language in which they can be spoken of is the language of paradox. But the statement may not be metaphysical at all; the reversal may be only a matter of nomenclature which leaves the absolute values of "fair" and "foul" unaffected. In that case, the statement is merely metalinguistic, and the problem the Weird Sisters raise (which now may be paraphrased, "That which has been called 'fair' will now be called 'foul' ") may conceivably be solved, not with the destruction of the rational universe, but with the revelation of the true order of things and the reimposition of a language actually descriptive of it.

"metalinguistic"

Of course there is no way of determining, simply on the basis of the Weird Sisters' formulation, which interpretation is correct: it is entirely to the point that both interpretations have to be entertained simultaneously. For the riddle "Fair is foul, and foul is fair," is, in miniature, the riddle of the play itself. The entire action of *Macbeth* similarly hovers between a metaphysical horror and a metalinguistic mistake: Has the order of Nature really been destroyed by Macbeth, so that "nothing is but what is not"? Or do "measure, time, and place" (those certainties to which Malcolm will appeal in the final speech) still encompass and control the apparent perversion of Macbeth's reign? Has the fantastic Scotland of Macbeth's ascendancy, where relations are inverted until "to do harm / Is often laudable, to do good sometime / Accounted dangerous folly" (IV.ii.74), become the image of some new metaphysical reality? Or will it prove merely a phantasm temporarily disguising the normal nature of Nature and "grace of Grace"?

In this *Macbeth*-world of apparently inherent ambiguity, the one perfectly unambiguous thing is the murder of Duncan. From the start it is conceived as just that: not sacrifice or revenge, but murder. We know from the start that the moral horror which is Duncan's murder cries out for retribution. Hence it is the murderer Macbeth's destiny that we most expectantly attend, and hence (in part) the unrelieved sense of inevitability and directness which gives *Macbeth* its distinctive dramatic concentration. And there is another cause, too, for this sense of concentration: in no other play does language so intimately and immediately reflect the action. Language in *Macbeth* is the mirror and even, in a sense, the cause of the extremity of the moral situation. Macbeth's deed is an overturning of normal values and relationships, and the language of the play (the Weird Sisters' speeches being only the most obvious examples) follows the action into the chaotic world he establishes, into the realm of impossibility, beyond the powers of ordinary conception, beyond the proper sphere of words.

[margin note: language as mirror, even cause of the extremity of the moral situation]

The world of Macbeth's ascendancy is pathological, a world in moral and physical extremity. A doctor attends helplessly upon the last hours of Macbeth and his lady, while Malcolm's forces (in league with those of England's gracious doctor-king) come to be "the med'cine of the sickly weal" which will effect their "country's purge" (V.ii.27). In Act I, Duncan announces his intention to "establish our estate upon / Our eldest, Malcolm" (I.iv.37); that ceremony, definitive of order and normal function, is forestalled by Macbeth, who stages in its place his own black counter-ritual of murder—a counter-ritual that becomes the basis for all the successive acts of unnaturalness which infect the *Macbeth*-world. Macbeth himself recognizes the sacred bonds his deed will cancel:

> He's here in double trust:
> First, as I am his kinsman and his subject—
> Strong both against the deed; then, as his host,
> Who should against his murderer shut the door,
> Not bear the knife myself.
>
> [I.vii.12]

After the murder, speaking hypocritically but (as Kenneth Muir puts it) with "the equivocation of the murderer who utters truth like lies," [4] Macbeth cries,

4. In Muir's Arden edition (London and Cambridge, Mass., 1951), p. xxx.

Had I but died an hour before this chance,
I had liv'd a blessed time; for, from this instant,
There's nothing serious in mortality—
All is but toys; renown and grace is dead;
The wine of life is drawn, and the mere lees
Is left this vault to brag of.

                              [II.iii.89]

The murder of Duncan makes "a breach in nature / For ruin's wasteful entrance" (II.iii.112); it is, as Macduff says, confusion's masterpiece, a "sacrilegious murder" (II.iii.65). The prodigies seen by Ross and the Old Man—darkness entombing the face of earth, a falcon destroyed by a mousing owl, horses "turn'd wild in nature" which devour each other—are the sympathic convulsions of a universe whose principle of order has been lost. " 'Tis unnatural, / Even like the deed that's done" (II.iv.10).

Examples of the unnaturalness of the language which reflects the unnaturalness of the deed are so numerous as to be almost a critical embarrassment: once it is noticed, it is heard echoing on almost every page—and (it had better be said) on the pages of several of the play's best critics. Francis Fergusson, for instance (whose theoretical stance enables him to relate languages and action most fully), begins a discussion of the play with Macbeth's lines justifying the killing of Duncan's grooms: "The expedition of my violent love / Outran the pauser reason" (II.iii.109). Fergusson writes: "It is the phrase, 'to outrun the pauser, reason,' which seems to me to describe the action, or motive, of the play as a whole. . . . To 'outrun' reason suggests an impossible stunt, like lifting oneself by one's own bootstraps. It also suggests a competition or race, like those of nightmare, which cannot be won." [5]

This "paradoxical striving beyond reason" is echoed elsewhere; Fergusson draws examples from the Witches' scene (which we have already looked at), and from the bleeding-sergeant scene:

5. "*Macbeth* as the Imitation of an Action," in *The Human Image in Dramatic Literature* (Garden City, N.Y., 1957), pp. 117-18.

> Doubtful it stood,
> As two spent swimmers that do cling together
> And choke their art;
>
> > [I.ii.7]
>
> . . . .
>
> So from that spring whence comfort seem'd to come
> Discomfort swells;
>
> > [27]
>
> . . . .
>
> Confronted him with self-comparisons,
> Point against point rebellious, arm 'gainst arm;
>
> > [56]
>
> . . . .
>
> What he hath lost, noble Macbeth hath won.
>
> > [end]

Another description of Macbeth's "irrational stunt" is his line, "I have no spur / To prick the sides of my intent, but only / Vaulting ambition, which o'er-leaps itself, / And falls on th' other" (I.vii.25); while from the Porter scene Fergusson cites a series of "lewd physical analogies for outrunning reason: drink as tempting lechery into a hopeless action; himself as wrestling with drink." [6]

antithesis   One of the rhetorical devices at work in these examples is antithesis (comfort-discomfort, lost-won). In the opinion of Kenneth Muir, the device marks "one of the predominant characteristics of the general style of the play—it consists of multitudinous antitheses." The Porter's words on lechery Muir takes as the most concentrated example of the device; he cites, "*provokes-unprovokes; provokes-takes away; desire-performance; makes-mars; sets on-takes off; persuades-disheartens; stand to-not stand to.*" Again, the stylistic device is seen as a direct embodiment of a central thematic concern; Muir writes, "We may link this trick of style with the 'wrestling of destruction with creation' which Mr. Wilson Knight has found in the

6. Fergusson, *The Human Image*, p. 120.

play, and with the opposition he has pointed out between night and day, life and death, grace and evil." [7]

Muir relates the antithetical style to yet another thematic-stylistic feature: "The opposition between the hand and the other organs and senses recurs again and again." [8] Macbeth speaks of the firstlings of his heart becoming the firstlings of his hand (IV.i.147; the line recalls, too, Lady Macbeth's willingness to pluck a different sort of firstling from her breast), and of the strange things in head "that will to hand, / Which must be acted ere they may be scann'd" (III.iv.139).

The history of that curiously objectified hand, and of Lady Macbeth's, is the history of their sin and its retribution. Of the many references to it—references which grow in hallucinatory horror as the murderous hand detaches itself from the murderers, finally to turn upon them—I can pause to cite only a few. Macbeth bids "the eye wink at the hand" (I.iv.52), much as Lady Macbeth hopes that her knife will not "see" the wound it makes (I.v.49). After the murder, his hands are "a sorry sight" and "hangman's hands," bearing (as Lady Macbeth says) "filthy witness" to the deed. In the same scene (II.ii) the hands return to "pluck out mine eyes," and Macbeth realizes that "all great Neptune's ocean" will not wash away the blood (60). Shortly after, Lady Macbeth will appear sleepwalking, obsessively washing her "little hand," while Mavbeth, too, feels "his secret murders sticking on his hands" (V.2.17).

The Doctor's comment on Lady Macbeth's sleepwalking, that it is "a great perturbation in nature, to receive at once the benefit of sleep and do the effects of watching" (V.i.9), suggests a sort of temporal dislocation closely related to those physical dislocations we notice in the matter of the disembodied hand. Such a temporal dislocation is more intensely suggested (through antithesis and the idea of outright conflict) in Macbeth's question, "What is the night?" and Lady Mac-

7. Arden ed., p. xxiii. Muir refers to G. Wilson Knight, *The Imperial Theme* (1931; 3d ed., London, 1951), p. 153.

8. Muir, p. xxxi.

beth's answer, "Almost at odds with morning, which is which"
(III.iv.126). In Lady Macbeth's address to her absent husband
we find a state in which the future is swallowed up by the
present:

> Thy letters have transported me beyond
> This ignorant present, and I feel now
> The future in the instant.
>
> [I.v.53]

But Macbeth himself has already experienced a similar,
though more frighteningly realized, state of temporal dislocation. "Present fears / Are less than horrible imaginings," he
discovers; and he goes on, describing this state which is
"Against the use of nature":

> My thought, whose murder yet is but fantastical,
> Shakes so my single state of man
> That function is smother'd in surmise,
> And nothing is but what is not.
>
> [I.iii.137]

The syntax of this remarkable speech is purposefully ambiguous. Not a thought *about* murder: rather, Macbeth's "murder" belongs to his "thought," as an already objective (and
yet still "fantastical" or imaginary) thing. And this objectifica-
tion of the purely imaginary gives a dangerous life to "murder": in its present effects upon Macbeth we see already how
the murder which is now possessed by thought may become, in
a quite different sense, the murder *of* thought—thought's destruction. This murder, which literally *is not*, threatens to become all and to reduce all to its state of nonexistence.

Elsewhere, Macbeth reverses the order of temporal dislocation as he attempts to make the present swallow up the future:

> If th' assassination
> Could trammel up the consequence, and catch,
> With his surcease, success; that but this blow
> Might be the be-all and the end-all here—

> But here upon this bank and shoal of time—
> We'd jump the life to come.
>
> [I.vii.2]

The desperateness of the attempt is reflected in the sounds of the line, as "success" seems virtually to leap out before "surcease" has died away—as Macbeth tries to make "surcease" *be* "success." Macbeth's attempt (as Cleanth Brooks has written) is "to conquer the future, an attempt involving him, like Oedipus, in a desperate struggle with fate itself." [9] That struggle is reflected in the sounds and rhythms of his speeches —those I have cited as well as others to be found in almost every scene of the play—speeches in which the sheer impossibility of Macbeth's project of evil finds its paradoxical expression.

No single rhetorical term will describe the style we have been examining. At times it appears as strict rhetorical antithesis; at times it is the hallucinatory antithesis of organ or sense dislocated and hypostatized. The style is only the most immediate expression of a struggle being fought out constantly in the play; Lady Macbeth says of Duncan's guards, for instance, "That death and nature do contend about them, / Whether they live or die" (II.ii.7). Frequently the style emerges more through the rhythms of the lines than strictly through the sense: Macbeth's "This supernatural soliciting / Cannot be ill; cannot be good" (I.iii.130) poses a dilemma but no real paradox, and yet the sounds of the line implicate it in the paradoxical mode. The style is frequent with Macbeth and Lady Macbeth but is certainly not confined to them; it affects all the characters, and conditions our response to their world, for it is the very image-in-sound of that world, where all coherence has apparently been destroyed and where, therefore, language is driven to the desperate expedients of paradox, antithesis, conundrum.

9. "The Naked Babe and the Cloak of Manliness," in *The Well-Wrought Urn* (New York, 1947), p. 38. See also G. I. Duthie, "Antithesis in *Macbeth*," *Shakespeare Survey* 19 (1966): 25–33.

These stylistic features, with the threat they reflect of the destruction of normal order, are sufficient to indicate the intimate connection between language and action in the play. But there is also another matter, leading into historical considerations, which can amplify that connection. I have in mind the matter of *equivocation:* Macbeth speaks of "th' equivocation of the fiend / That lies like truth" (V.v.43), while the Porter welcomes into hell "an equivocator, that could swear in both the scales against either scale; who committed treason enough for God's sake, yet could not equivocate to heaven" (II.iii.8). Now at several points in this study I have used the word *equivocation* to refer to the various kinds of linguistic or epistemological problems the tragedies confront; but here in *Macbeth* the word has a more precise, technical meaning.

Behind the references in *Macbeth* lie the Jesuit doctrine of equivocation and, most immediately, the Gunpowder Plot trials which brought that doctrine to wide public attention. It it possible, indeed, to see reflected generally in the play's atmosphere of terrors and intrigues some of the feelings that were aroused by the Gunpowder Plot— a plot which, in its wholesale attack upon the state's actual and symbolic principles of order, was an enactment of the age's obsessive nightmare, a bursting of the most fantastic horrors onto the stage of life. But for our purposes it is more important to notice how much the doctrine of equivocation involved a question of language and (from the non-Jesuit point of view) the implication of language in the propagation of evil.

The basis of the Jesuit doctrine, which was intended to accomplish the neat trick of saving both the lives and (at a later date) the souls of Catholics haled before English courts, has been extensively traced by Frank L. Huntley. It derived from Aristotle's characterization of "enunciative propositions" which could be either "spoken, or written, or thought, or mixed"—mixed so that (as Jesuit polemicists interpreted Aristotle) a true proposition could be framed that was in part spoken and in part only thought, "God being witness to the mind." A Catholic, even under solemn oath, could tell just half the truth to men so long as he told God (however silently) all of it. An example of how the doctrine could work is cited by Huntley from an anti-Jesuit tract of 1603:

> one demanding of you whether, if the Pope should come in warlike manner to invade this land by force of arms, you would take his part or the Queen's; you framing this answer in your mind, "we will take the Queen's part, if the Pope will command us to do so," may by their doctrine give this answer lawfully, *viz.* "we will take the Queen's part"—and conceal the rest; whereby he that asked the question is plainly deluded.[10]

At the trial of Father Garnet (the supposed prototype of the Porter's equivocator), Sir Edward Coke charged that the doctrine taught "not only simple lying, but fearful and damnable blasphemy." Certainly, as Coke must have felt acutely, it constituted an attack upon the basis of the entire judicial system. And further, as I think Shakespeare may have felt, it constituted an attack upon all the bases of rational discourse.

For the doctrine, with its all-purpose escape clause about "mental reservation," perverts the nature of language, which must be public and exoteric, into something private and esoteric.[11] A speech that is not spoken becomes as good as a speech that is spoken: the doctrine gives a sort of metaphysical warrant to solipsism, and elevates individual fantasy to a status equal with public reality. It is something like this which, I think, Shakespeare saw in the doctrine and is remembered in

10. *"Macbeth* and the Background of Jesuitical Equivocation," *PMLA* 79 (September 1964) : 396. See also Muir's introduction to the Arden edition, pp. xviii–xxi, and Henry N. Paul, *The Royal Play of "Macbeth"* (New York, 1950), pp. 237–47. David Kaula has produced evidence that Shakespeare was more intimately acquainted with Jesuit polemics than has been generally supposed; see, for instance, his *"Hamlet* and the *Sparing Discoverie," Shakespeare Survey* 24 (1971) : 71–77.

11. I borrow the opposition of "esoteric" versus "exoteric" in relation to the function of language from Geoffrey Hartman, "Structuralism: The Anglo-American Adventure," *Yale French Studies* 36–37 (1966; double issue) : 167.

much of the play's rhetoric, as well as in the specific references
to equivocation. Once the public certainties of language are
destroyed—and in *Macbeth* the Weird Sisters signal that destruction—the boundaries between the real and the fantastic
are down, and the way is open for the projected images of the
individual mind to overwhelm the objective world. Something
similar has already been seen in Iago's use of language, with
its ability to interpolate an obscene fantasy into the normal
waking world; and when we come to *King Lear* we will see
how specifically Shakespeare relates the dangers of a solipsistic language to actual madness.

The Weird Sisters are themselves the first visible manifesta-
tion of the confusion between public reality and private fantasy: "Are ye fantastical, or that indeed / Which outwardly ye
show?" Macbeth's introductory line, "So foul and fair a day
I have not seen," immediately demonstrates their power to infect others with their air of fantastic paradox; as Dowden
commented, "Their spells have already wrought upon his
blood." [12] Like the Weird Sisters' incantatory lines, Macbeth's
line is a riddle with an easy answer: it is a foul day because of
the weather, and fair because of the victory. But, again like
the Weird Sisters' lines, this simple explanation does not entirely dissolve the residual paradox the rhetoric suggests. From
the very first, Macbeth is a willing accomplice in helping to
fantasticate his world into the unreal and the unreasonable.

The doctrine of equivocation, I have suggested, tried to
justify a potentially dangerous confusion between thought and
speech. It could not have been a difficult step for Shakespeare
to generalize from that confusion to Macbeth's habit of con-
fusing thought with *action,* a habit of mind which signals
Macbeth's first major contribution to the irruption of unreality. The process begins with Macbeth's "rapt" reflections
on the "happy prologues to the swelling act / Of the imperial
theme" (I.iii.128). The "suggestion" of a possible future action, its "horrid image," already has power to disturb Macbeth "Against the use of nature," until "function is smother'd

12. Quoted by Muir, Arden ed., p. 15, n. 38.

hypostatization of thought

in surmise, / And nothing is but what is not" (140). The imagined future, as I have already observed, overwhelms the present reality.

Most strikingly, the "thought" itself becomes a "murder": as to the Jesuitical equivocators a thought could be a speech, so to Macbeth a thought can be a deed. The hypostatization of thought will become characteristic of Macbeth; and the casting out of that clamorous thought into the realm of action will become an obsessive concern with him. He will have to rip his thought out of himself with the sort of ferocity Lady Macbeth reserves for the infant at her breast: "From this moment / The very firstlings of my heart shall be / The firstlings of my hand. . . . be it thought and done" (IV.i.146). The normal order of thought and action becomes reversed: "Strange things I have in head that will to hand, / That must be acted ere they may be scann'd" (III. iv. 139). Compulsive action must exorcise obsessive thought.

The hypostatization of thought recurs: "Stars, hide your fires," Macbeth prays; "Let not light see my black and deep *desires*" (I.iv.50). It recurs most terrifyingly as the dagger covered with "gouts of blood": the "dagger of the mind," though a "false creation," points Macbeth the way to Duncan's chamber (II.i.33 ff.). The rhetorical confusion has now invaded the sphere of action; the mere thought has become "in form as palpable" as the real dagger Macbeth draws. Now the murder, which Macbeth's fantasy, overwhelming the actual present, had interpolated into the objective world, also becomes a visible presence; now "wither'd murder . . . thus with his stealthy pace, / With Tarquin's ravishing strides, towards his design / Moves like a ghost" (II.i.52). Or it moves, "thus," like Macbeth himself, for Macbeth both watches the "wither'd murder" and also *is* it. Hallucination and reality blend.

Finally, the unreal which Macbeth's rhetoric has helped to summon into the real world becomes master over the real. The "horrible shadow," the "unreal mockery," of Banquo's ghost stands before Macbeth demanding blood, mute witness to the destruction of natural process Macbeth has wrought:

The time has been
That when the brains were out the man would die,
And there an end; but now they rise again,
With twenty mortal murders on their crowns,
And push us from our stools.

[III.iv.78]

Macbeth's impossible project fails: he has not exorcised intolerable thought, but only turned it loose into the world
whence it may return to plague the inventor.

Macbeth's thought, like the world he helps bring to birth,
is unnatural, dominated by the horror of nothingness. But now
the fully paradoxical quality of that nothingness is revealed,
for as it turns on Macbeth and begins his destruction, we
realize that unnaturalness itself is finally at the service of
nature, of the natural. Now this statement demands some
examination, for it has about it, I fear, the ring of an overly
neat formulation, reducing complex issues of morality and
theology, as well as of dramatic structure, to a turn of phrase.
How can unnaturalness serve nature, and nothingness be its
own destruction? These questions are related to one raised
earlier; whether the perverted Scotland of Macbeth's ascendancy represents a new order of things, in which fair and foul
have indeed changed places, or whether behind that apparent
inversion there subsists still a normal order that will attest to
evil's essential insubstantiality (its "nothingness"). I began this
chapter with a quotation from Boethius; here I will turn to
him again because his *Consolation* bears closely on the questions at hand: both *Macbeth* and *The Consolation of Philosophy* confront directly the question of evil and the problems
raised by the existence of evil for one who assumes that the
universe is a divinely ordered affair.

Boethius's Lady Philosophy draws a distinction between Fate
and Providence. The definitions of these two words are worth
quoting at some length:

> The generation of all things, and the whole course of
> mutable natures and of whatever is in any way subject to

change, take their causes, order, and forms from the unchanging mind of God. This divine mind established the manifold rules by which all things are governed while it remained in the secure castle of its own simplicity. When this government is regarded as belonging to the purity of the divine mind, it is called Providence [*prouidentia nominatur*]; but when it is considered with reference to the things which it moves and governs, it has from very early times been called Fate [*fatum a ueteribus appellatum est*]. It is easy to see that Providence and Fate are different if we consider the power of each. Providence is the divine reason itself which belongs to the most high ruler of all things and which governs all things; Fate, however, belongs to all mutable things and is the disposition by which Providence joins all things in their own order. For Providence embraces all things equally, however diverse they are, however infinite. Fate, on the other hand, sets particular things in motion once they have been given their own forms, places, and times. Thus Providence is the unfolding of temporal events as this is present to the vision of the divine mind; but this same unfolding of events as it is worked out in time is called Fate. Although the two are different things, one depends upon the other, for the process of Fate derives from the simplicity of Providence. Just as the craftsman conceives in his mind the form of the thing he intends to make, and then sets about making it by producing in successive temporal acts that which was simply present in his mind, so God by his Providence simply and unchangeably disposes all things that are to be done, even though the things themselves are worked out by Fate in many ways and in the process of time. [Book IV, Prose 6] [13]

As we watch Shakespeare's play unfold in time we watch the workings of Fate—and it may not be irrelevant to recall here that the Weird Sisters' name derives from the Old English

13. *Consolation of Philosophy,* pp. 91–92.

wyrd, subject
to Providence
(a Boethian gloss
of a Nordic
myth)

wyrd, or "fate." But "everything which is subject to Fate is subject also to Providence and . . . Fate itself is also subject to Providence." And the playwright nowhere better justifies the analogy between himself as "maker" and the Divine Maker than in his ability to reveal, along with the temporal workings of Fate, the immutable Providence behind it. As we contemplate the perfected form of his tragedy, we stand at the still point and can see the providential order within which Fate takes its apparently capricious course.

We may consider the matter from an esthetic point of view: as audience we feel a certain assurance about the outcome of the drama and a sense of fitness when it is achieved; or from a theological one: the faithful know that evil itself is subject to and must ultimately serve the Providence beyond Fate. Either way, we find in *Macbeth* an apparent doubleness which, in the revealed stillness of the completed tragedy, is resolved into the most purely natural simplicity. We find a struggle between good and evil, the natural and the unnatural, in which (without any diminution of the horrors of evil) both sides ultimately serve the same end.

In the prophecies of Fate we can see how the unnatural serves the natural. When Macbeth receives the promise that he "shall never vanquished be until / Great Birnam Wood to high Dunsinane Hill / Shall come against him" (IV.i.92), he replies confidently:

> That will never be.
> Who can impress the forest, bid the tree
> Unfix his earth-bound root? Sweet bodements, good!
> Rebellion's head rise never till the wood
> Of Birnam rise, and our high-plac'd Macbeth
> Shall live the lease of nature, pay his breath
> To time and mortal custom.
>
> [94]

Macbeth will live out his natural life, that is, because it is unnatural that Birnam Wood should rise. But Birnam Wood does rise, and it does so in the most natural way. The action of the play here imitates its language, for the simple military strategy that brings Birnam Wood to Dunsinane is an action natural and reasonable, just as, despite the apparent paradoxes, the Weird Sisters in Act I, Scene 1 had said nothing that was not finally natural and reasonable. The hint of something bathetic in the Weird Sisters, something even silly in their doggerel attempts to sound frightening, is repeated in the bathos of their prophecy's fulfillment: like all their riddles, it had a simple solution.

And indeed "Macbeth / Shall live the lease of nature, pay his breath / To time and mortal custom." Nowhere is the play's irony, born of that vision which sees at once the temporal workings of Fate and the immutability of the Providence beyond it, more subtle than in these lines. For the destroyer of order to fulfill nature's lease, paying his breath to time and mortal custom, is for the destroyer to be destroyed: mankind's hope is the monster's doom. "Tomorrow, and tomorrow, and tomorrow, / Creeps in this petty pace from day to day"; but only for Macbeth is that grinding progression toward dusty death a cause for despair. For the rest of Scotland, the orderly progression of tomorrow following tomorrow following tomorrow is testimony to the existence of an order which guarantees the end of Macbeth's reign of evil and the restoration of nature's good.

The success of Macbeth's project depended upon his ability to dislocate the normal progression of time, to feel the future in the instant and trammel it there. But such a trammeling exists only at the divinely still center, while "whatever strays farthest from the divine mind is most entangled in the nets of Fate" (*Consolation*, Book IV, Prose 6). And thus we notice that, alongside the many references in the play to time's dislocation, there have also been from the beginning assurances that an orderly tomorrow must come.

Macbeth himself, ironically enough, first enunciates the promise that "Come what come may, / Time and the hour runs through the roughest day" (I.iii.146). Following Duncan's murder, Malcolm declares, "This murderous shaft that's

shot / Hath not yet lighted" (II.iii.140): he means, of course,
that it may yet light on him, but to the audience that attends
the downfall of Macbeth, the line may also describe the sort
of action which bespeaks orderly natural process. The curious
scene in Act 4, scene 3, where Malcolm first condemns himself
and then retracts the condemnation (thus enacting the resolution of doubleness into simplicity), concludes with an assertion of time's orderly progression and an appeal to natural
ripeness:

> Macbeth
> Is ripe for shaking, and the pow'rs above
> Put on their instruments. Receive what cheer you may;
> The night is long that never finds the day.
>
> [IV.iii.237]

And finally Macduff is able to announce the death of the
tyrant with the declaration, "The time is free" (V.viii.55).

The Weird Sisters say that "Fair is foul, and foul is fair,"
and on the literal truth of that paradoxical inversion Macbeth
rests his career. The statement is, in fact, not strictly an
equivocation, but rather (as the Jesuit apologists would have
recognized) a case of amphibology, a statement susceptible to
various interpretations. One interpretation is the metaphysical: evil and good have really changed places; another is the
metalinguistic: only names and appearances have changed.
The latter interpretation is virtually given in the play; it is
Malcolm's assertion of the "rule in unity":

> That which you are, my thoughts cannot transpose;
> Angels are bright still, though the brightest fell.
> Though all things foul would wear the brows of grace,
> Yet grace must still look so.
>
> [IV.iii.21]

The prophecies are fulfilled—literally and quite naturally,
the woods rise against Dunsinane—and with this reinversion of
paradoxical inversion, the world and the language that describes it are once more in accord. The action of the play

resolves itself as the riddles of the play's language resolve themselves. Elsewhere in this study we have seen how the formal resolution of a tragedy may be only partially in accord with its thematic resolution, or even (in *Troilus and Cressida*) how formal discord may cast doubt upon the very possibility of resolution. But in *Macbeth,* more I think than in any other of Shakespeare's tragedies, the form of the play triumphantly asserts its thematic, moral resolution. The phantasm of evil recedes and the normal order of life reemerges, as Malcolm promises, "by the grace of Grace" to "perform in measure, time, and place" the ritual of coronation, of natural succession, which Macbeth had temporarily forestalled.

7

Coriolanus

In *Othello* and *Macbeth* we saw language used imaginatively but also perversely. In *Othello,* we looked at the relationship between a lying fable and the fable that tells essential truth; in *Macbeth,* at the unnaturalness of evil as it is embodied in a language of inversions and paradox. Now, in examining *Coriolanus,* it may seem that we are turning away from the imaginative use of language in almost any form: the peculiar stylistic barrenness (compared to the poetic richness of the previous plays), the narrowness of its "range of tone and feeling," [1] is one of the most frequently remarked characteristics of *Coriolanus.* And the hero of the play may also seem out of place in this study: I have located as a primary impetus for tragic action a man's need to achieve self-expression; however, Coriolanus is not only the least eloquent of Shakespeare's tragic figures but one who (as we shall see) specifically rejects that humanizing speech sought by Titus or Hamlet.

Coriolanus is in these ways exceptional. In another way, however, it is perfectly Shakespearean, for in this play, as much as in *Macbeth,* style and theme (those handily abstractions we use for discursive analysis) are inextricably united. The almost hallucinatory metaphoric richness of *Macbeth* is the linguistic embodiment of its action; the apparently bare style of *Coriolanus* is, similarly, the fitting language for its quite different action. And as we can trace the action of *Macbeth* through an examination of its peculiar rhetoric, so we can trace the action of *Coriolanus*—only here we can be more specific about the

1. D. J. Enright, "*Coriolanus:* Tragedy or Debate," *Essays in Criticism* 4 (1954) : 4.

particular rhetorical device at issue. The stylistic peculiarity of *Coriolanus* comes very largely from the unusual prominence given to metonymy and synecdoche—modes of expression directly related to the nature of the thing to be expressed.[2]

To say that metonymy and synecdoche, rather than the more customary metaphor and simile, are the most prominent rhetorical figures in *Coriolanus* is not, I am aware, the most exciting of all possible observations. But there is reason to believe that the distinction between metonymy and metaphor is of more fundamental significance than might at first appear, and shortly I will be offering evidence to support the claim. The distinction is of importance to theories of poetry in general, but here I will be concerned only with its significance for *Coriolanus*. And as a first step in relating the figure of metonymy to the themes of the play, we may note that metonymy and synecdoche are figures of fragmentation and usurpation—of parts representing the whole and of the whole absorbing its parts; and that *Coriolanus* is a play about the relationship of the individual to the community, of the community to its constituent members, and of the association of man with man, and of man with the elements that compound him.

Coriolanus is a world of "fragments" (the epithet is directed by Caius Marcius Coriolanus at the common people of Rome), populated not by men but by parts of men. A "great toe" is bid to address an assembly of "scabs" (I.i.153, 164), a youthful warrior's "Amazonian chin" drives "the bristled lips before

2. I take "metonymy" (the use of the name of one thing to represent another thing with which it is associated) as the general term, reserving "synecdoche" (the part for the whole, the species for the genus, etc.) for more specialized cases. Examples of "the thing contained for the container" are rare, but notable is the contribution James Thurber made in his studies with Miss Groby: "If a woman were to grab up a bottle of Grade A and say to her husband, 'Get away from me or I'll hit you with the milk,' that would be a Thing Contained for the Container" (*The Thurber Carnival* [New York, 1945], p. 53). Thanks to Prof A. Walter Litz for recalling it to my attention.

him" (II.ii.89), the tribunes of the people are "the tongues
o' th' common mouth" (III.i.22). Repeatedly, parts or functions
of men are made to stand for the whole: men give their
"voices" (that is, their votes); but also they *are* merely voices,
disembodied, autonomous, grotesque. (But the returning hero
hails his wife as his "gracious silence" [II.i.166].) The epithet
voices comes quite naturally; the word had, in Elizabethan
usage, the technical meaning of "votes," and was so used by
North in translating Plutarch.[3] But in Act II, scene 3, where
Coriolanus must humble himself before the people and sue
to them for their "voices," the act and the actor are made
contemptuously synonymous. The people's role in the state,
according to Coriolanus, is merely to give their voices as they
are directed (although when they overstep themselves they do
clamor hungrily for other oral gratifications), and so they become no more than gaping mouths and noisy voices; they are,
as Coriolanus mockingly addresses them, "most sweet voices,"
"worthy voices!" (109, 134). Such frequently repeated reductive images as these create in the play a grotesquerie of partial
beings distorted into impossible positions: a warrior, for instance, must display himself by displaying his wounds, and
the grateful people "are to put [their] tongues into those
wounds and speak for them" (II.iii.6).

   In a play so rich in vituperation as *Coriolanus,* it is not
surprising to find these reductive images, but for their frequently metonymic character some explanation is necessary.
And one is not far to seek: the play's numerous and striking
metonymies are conditioned—in effect called into being—by
Menenius's fable of the body and the belly. There is, I think,

---

3. Several writers have commented on the use of *voice* in the play:
see especially Leonard F. Dean, "Voice and Deed in *Coriolanus," University of Kansas City Review* 21 (1955): 177–84; Norman Rabkin, *Shakespeare and the Common Understanding* (New York, 1967), pp. 134–35. (According to Dean, *voice* occurs forty-six times in the play; according to
Rabkin, forty-one; Martin Spevak, *A Complete and Systematic Concord-
ance to the Works of Shakespeare,* Vol. 3 [Hildesheim, 1968], gives twelve
instances of *voice* and thirty-six of *voices.*)

no other play in which Shakespeare so clearly allows a single image to dominate. The fable, slowly and amusingly developed by the garrulous patrician in Act I, scene 1, largely determines the nature of the succeeding imagery, and determines it in the direction of metonymy.

Menenius's "pretty tale" is, as he is content to remark, hardly new. The state is like a man: in both state and man, health depends upon the cooperation of all the members and organs, each of which must perform its allotted task. Thus the smiling belly of Menenius's fable reminds "th' discontented members, the mutinous parts" (I.i.109) of the body that, although he receives "the general food at first," he does so only to distribute it to his "incorporate friends" (128–29). (And thus the well-fed patricians are supposed to do for the hungry plebeians.) The very commonplace nature of this little moral tale is all to Shakespeare's purpose; it is only a special application of the universally known correspondence of microcosm and macrocosm—a correspondence so simple (yet inclusive) that, once established by Menenius thus early in the play, it can continue to preside over the play's imagery till the end.

We are, in a sense, imprisoned within the limits of vision the fable establishes; we remain within its frame of reference, where, whether our attention is directed to the individual man or to the world at large, we see before us the human body, its parts at war one with the other. The dominance of the image gains for the play a simplifying clarity, but loses the complicating expansiveness characteristic of metaphor. For Menenius's fable is not a metaphor but an extended metonymy; it is, indeed, an instance of what Kenneth Burke (in his somewhat specialized vocabulary) describes as "the 'noblest synecdoche,' the perfect paradigm or prototype of all lesser usages, [which] is found in metaphysical doctrines proclaiming the identity of 'microcosm' and 'macrocosm.' In such doctrines," writes Burke, "where the individual is seen as a replica of the universe, and vice versa, we have the ideal synecdoche, since microcosm is related to macrocosm as part to whole, and either the whole can represent the part or the part can repre-

sent the whole." [4] In *Coriolanus,* once Menenius has established his version of this prototypic metonymy, defining for
us the macrocosm of Rome both in its present dissentient
reality and in its unrealized ideal of order, the microcosmic
metonymies follow inevitably: finishing his tale, Menenius
turns to the First Citizen and asks, "What do you think, / You,
the great toe of this assembly?" (I.i.152).

In the midst of Rome's fragmentary citizens, its mere parts
of men loudly demanding the rights of whole men, stands
Coriolanus—indivisibly whole, heroically complete, refusing
(but, as we shall see, in vain) any division of his essence. With
monolithic integrity Coriolanus denies in himself those con-
tradictions (or, from another point of view, complexities)
which mark lesser mortals. Over and over, this distinction is
drawn between Coriolanus and the self-divided rabble which
surrounds him: the people "can yield [their voices] now / And
straight disclaim their tongues" (III.i.34); they have bodies
without hearts and tongues which "cry / Against the rectorship
of judgment" (II.iii.201); the tribunes have "ears and eyes for
th' time, / But hearts for the event" (II.i.259)—but Caius Marcius is the man whose "heart's his mouth; / What his breast
forges, that his tongue must vent" (III.i.257). Unlike his enemies, Coriolanus is integrated, all-of-a-piece; heart, mouth,
breast, and tongue work together to one end—an end, it may
be noted, of almost inhuman simplicity.

Coriolanus's insistence upon singular wholeness sets him
apart even from his fondest allies. Indeed, it is his mother
Volumnia, in Act III (as once again, and fatally, she will do
in Act V), who most effectively condemns her son's impossible
ideal. Coriolanus cannot understand why Volumnia would
have him act other than as his heart bids: "Why did you wish
me milder? Would you have me / False to my nature? Rather
say I play / The man I am" (III.ii.14). To follow Volumnia's
politic advice would be to accept in himself that state of
fragmentation he despises in others:

4. "Appendix D: Four Master Tropes," *A Grammar of Motives* (1945;
republished together with *A Rhetoric of Motives,* Cleveland, 1962), p. 508.

Must I go show them my unbarb'd sconce? Must I
With my base tongue give to my noble heart
A lie that it must bear?

. . . .

 I will not do't,
Lest I surcease to honour mine own truth,
And by my body's action teach my mind
A most inherent baseness.

[III.ii.99, 120]

But such indeed is Volumnia's advice, and she will herself provide the example:

Pray be counsell'd;
I have a heart as little apt as yours,
But yet a brain that leads my use of anger
To better vantage.

[III.ii.28]

With heart thus divided from brain, Coriolanus must force himself to speak "such words that are but roted in / Your tongue, though but bastards and syllables / Of no allowance to your bosom's truth" (55).

We may question the ultimate moral value of Volumnia's counsel, but her urging does redress, if only too humanly, the inhumanity of Coriolanus's posture. Inhuman, for Coriolanus's demands, upon himself and others, go beyond even the ideal of harmony defined in Menenius's fable. By the logic of the Microcosm-macrocosm analogy, the individual as well as the state is made up of disparate parts: the parts may, at best, work in easy cooperation, but to deny (as Coriolanus would do) one's essentially fragmentary nature is to deny one's humanness.

The body-synecdoches which describe the common people would never do to describe Coriolanus, and indeed there come to be attached to him metonymies of another sort that turn him from a human being into (in G. Wilson Knight's apt phrase) "a slaying machine of mechanic excellence." [5] Before

5. *The Imperical Theme* (London, 1931), p. 168.

Corioli, "from face to foot / He was a thing of blood, whose
every motion / Was tim'd with dying cries" (II.ii.106). The
whole man is fused so immediately with his function that he
is not merely a warrior but the embodied shape of war itself:
"Death, that dark spirit, in's nervy arm doth lie, / Which,
being advanc'd, declines, and then men die" (II.i.151). His
obsessive drive for simple wholeness of being is most perfectly
expressed when his jubilant soldiers, shouting and waving
their caps, "take him up in their arms," and Coriolanus cries
with the ecstacy of fulfillment, "O, me alone! Make you a
sword of me?" (I.vi.76).

What Coriolanus denies in himself, he despises in the state
and would extirpate—its fragmentary, representative nature,
its at least partial democracy of functions. Thus far he is
faithful to Menenius's analogy: he is a totalitarian both of the
emotions and of the body politic. On the political level, it may
be noted, Rome's very form of government is a type of
metonymy; again, the general observation is Kenneth Burke's:

> A . . . synecdochic form is present in all theories of politi-
> cal representation, where some part of the social body
> (either traditionally established, or elected, or coming
> into authority by revolution) is held to be "representative"
> of the society as a whole. . . . [I]n a complex civilization
> any act of representation automatically implies a synec-
> dochic relationship (insofar as the act is, or is held to be,
> "truly representative").[6]

But Coriolanus, who despises the man whose mouth speaks
other than as his heart prompts, whose every function is not
knit into one machine-perfect instrument for achievement,
cannot brook such synecdochic representation—in Rome, a
synecdoche that leaves the "voice" grotesquely dominant over
the whole. He cannot brook it, at any rate, unless he is the
part that stands for the whole. The quarrel between Coriolanus and the people is thus made fully irreconcilable precisely over the question of a synecdoche: "Where is this viper /
That would depopulate the city and / Be every man himself?"

6. *Grammar of Motives*, p. 508.

demands the tribune Sicinius (III.i.263) and: "What is the city but the people?"—to which the people's answer comes, "True, / The people are the city" (III.i.199). And Coriolanus's response is as clear and consistent: one man alone, he turns upon his assembled judges and cries, "I banish you" (III.iii. 125).

Perhaps the oddest, certainly one of the most revealing, aspects of Coriolanus's demand for wholeness of being is his distrust of words, and indeed of all the conventional symbolic means (verbal and gestural) that men have for expressing themselves. For all his vituperation, it is the refusal to speak —to exhort his men kindly, to acknowledge their praise, to show his wounds (a sort of silent speech), to answer Aufidius's accusations—which is most characteristic of him. In fact, the disastrous refusal to show his wounds to the people also suggests the reason for Coriolanus's antipathy to the conventional arts of language: it is a refusal to allow parts to speak for his whole.

And so with all language, and especially the language of explanation and self-definition: the very words and gestures by which men make their meanings apparent, which *stand for* us, are implicated in that self-divisiveness against which Coriolanus struggles, are things (as Coriolanus sees it) apart from us that come, basely, to represent us. Coriolanus, we know, cannot flatter or hear flattery spoken of him—but beyond that we are left with the impression that he simply cannot speak; for to accept words in place of the whole man is to be like the common people, "the wisdom of [whose] choice is rather to have my hat than my heart" (II.iii.97). Cominius describes the only mode of communication, of mediation between himself and the world, which Coriolanus can approve: Coriolanus, he says, "rewards / His deeds with doing them, and is content / To spend the time to end it" (II.ii.125). No discursive substitute or memorial ceremony, but only the man in action, the thing itself, can suffice. Only in the instant when man and deed are totally united in the act that defines the man is he adequately expressed; only when Coriolanus *is* his sword is Coriolanus wholly manifested.

Coriolanus's uneasiness over the arts of language is in a way reminiscent of Hamlet's struggle with the problem of self-expression. Hamlet, in Act I, finding himself in a world of seeming, disdains (like Coriolanus) all the "actions that a man might play," and therefore is deprived of "all forms, moods, shapes of grief" that could denote him truly. His whole allegiance is, initially, to "that within which passes show." And Coriolanus too, like Hamlet, relates hypocrisy to the histrionic: "Would you have me / False to my nature?" we have heard him demand of Volumnia; "rather say I play / The man I am." His protest against "playing" is buttressed by the venerable platonic charge that the feigning of drama or poetry may lead to a blurring of the lines between role and reality, or to an outright usurpation of the one by the other. Coriolanus will not play any part but "the man I am," "Lest I surcease to honour mine own truth, / And by my body's action teach my mind / A most inherent baseness."

But these similarities between Hamlet and Coriolanus cannot be more than superficial. For Hamlet, under the exigencies of his situation and with the aid of a troop of professional actors, discovers a way to unite histrionic action with the action that is immediate being. Coriolanus, on the other hand, never unites the two senses of acting. Instead, we find him confronted with a paradox he is quite incapable of resolving, that the actions he undertakes in order to be most true to "the man I am" lead him to a baseness least like his ideal of selfhood.

In proper names, that class of words whose special function it is to represent us, we find the paradox most clearly revealed. Cominius (who, though a soldier, is as easy with language as Coriolanus is uneasy with it) seems to have found an acceptable formula: the one appropriate gesture the army can offer its hero is to bestow upon him a name which most nearly identifies the doer with his deeds:

> and from this time,
> For what he did before Corioli, call him

> With all th' applause and clamour of the host,
> Caius Marcius Coriolanus.
> Bear th' addition nobly ever!
>
> [I.ix.62]

The name is informed immediately with its occasion and is close enough to the wordless integrity Coriolanus would prefer. But still it is only words, still a synecdoche standing inadequately for the whole man. And the history of Coriolanus's name, its acquisition and its loss, is a history that reveals the impossible nature of its bearer's quest to be heroically self-constituted.

For the bestowing of a name, especially one so intrinsically related to its bearer as "Coriolanus," is a social act, defining relationships, going outside of whatever purely inner integrity we can conceive. Now everything Coriolanus does is done to be true to himself, but everything he does after his break with Rome—the Rome which named him and so largely defines his being—proves him a traitor not only to Rome but to himself. He believes he is true to himself even in making his alliance with Aufidius; that is, given the man Caius Marcius Coriolanus, this new alliance is the one he must make: but that name remains to show that in being thus true to "himself," he is being false to another self who is a son, a husband, a father, a Roman.

The new alliance makes his name an anomaly, and as early as his first appearance before Aufidius it is felt to be an embarrassing impediment; to Aufidius's repeated demand, "Speak, man. What's thy name?" he at last replies:

> If, Tullus,
> Not yet thou know'st me, and, seeing me, dost not
> Think me for the man I am, necessity
> Commands me name myself.
>
> [IV.v.54]

The name remains, but not its meaning; the relationships of honor and of enmity that it implied are being overturned:

My name is Caius Marcius, who hath done
To thee particularly, and to all the Volsces,
Great hurt and mischief; thereto witness may
My surname, Coriolanus. The painful service,
The extreme dangers, and the drops of blood
Shed for my thankless country, are requited
But with that surname—a good memory
And witness of the malice and displeasure
Which thou shouldst bear me. Only that name re-
    mains. . . .

                                        [IV.v.65]

The name that once defined him as closely as a name can do,
has now become a measure of the distance its bearer has
traveled from himself, from his own identity. It is a state which
cannot be allowed to endure, and shortly we have Cominius's
report:

                'Coriolanus'
He would not answer to; forbad all names;
He was a kind of nothing, titleless,
Till he had forg'd himself a name i' th' fire
Of burning Rome.

                                        [V.i.11]

The loss of his name in the pursuit of an ideal of integrity
reveals the full irony of Coriolanus's career. Now he must remain "a kind of nothing, titleless," or else forge a new name
in a new social relationship—but one that makes him a traitor
to the man he was.

    The question of selfhood I have been discussing is not one,
it must be admitted, which Coriolanus, the least introspective
of Shakespearean heroes, thinks much about. To him, rather,
the question appears to be one more appropriate to soldiers,
the question of manhood. And it is therefore curious, but
also appropriate, that we learn more about the *childhood* of
this insistently heroic man than we do about the childhood of
any other of Shakespeare's tragic heroes. The play's domestic

emphasis is vastly important: it leads directly to Aufidius's taunt, "Boy!" and to Coriolanus's destruction. Volumnia is, of course, the person most responsible for her son's striving toward heroic manhood (and it is a large part of the play's irony that, as the First Citizen astutely recognizes, much of Coriolanus's drive for self-sufficiency results from his need "to please his mother" [I.i.38]); Volumnia, who, when her young son came home wounded from battle, "sprang not more in joy at first hearing he was a man-child than now in first seeing he had proved himself a man" (I.iii.18). And hearing Volumnia, and seeing the results of her training in her ferocious son, we are forced to recognize how the desire to prove oneself a man can imply, in fact, the desire to be less than— or at least other than—a fully sentient human being. When Macduff hears how Macbeth has slaughtered his family, he is told to bear it like a man. He replies that he must also *feel* it like a man: that is a sort of manhood Coriolanus knows nothing about.

To be a man, as Coriolanus understands it, is to be sufficient and whole in a way no man in fact can be. But to be a "boy" is eminently human: the boy's very incompleteness implies the contingency of a human state. And in *Coriolanus* the boy is always present before us, contained in, or superimposed upon, the man he has become. Presenting young Marcius to his father, Volumnia says, "This is a poor epitome of yours, / Which by th' interpretation of full time / May show like all yourself" (V.iii.68); this is another instance of microcosm and macrocosm, and the reflection works both ways: in the man Coriolanus we see the boy Caius Marcius.

And we have seen him from the start: "O' my word, the father's son" (I.iii.57), Valeria declares, as she describes how young Marcius "mammock'd" a butterfly; and that childish image is never far away as we watch the grown man in his rage, mammocking his human enemies. The two sets of images—boy and butterfly, man and enemy—come together in Cominius's description of Coriolanus: the Volscian soldiers, he says, "follow him / Against us brats with no less confidence / Than boys pursuing summer butterflies" (IV.vi.93). And at the beginning of Act V, scene 4 the image, subtly varied now, makes a last appearance. The subject under discussion is Coriolanus's inflexible enmity to Rome: "Is't possible that so short a time can alter the condition of a man?" asks Sicinius. And Menenius replies: "There is difference between a grub and a butterfly; yet your butterfly was a grub. This Marcius is grown from man to dragon; he has wings, he's more than a creeping thing."

Here the image is used to demonstrate Coriolanus's emergence as the mature destroyer of Rome, but again we cannot help recalling the boy who "mammock'd" a butterfly. Only now, by a remarkable compression of the image, Coriolanus *is* the butterfly—and a butterfly who has been a grub; the image reminds us that Coriolanus was a boy (a "grub"), has grown, did change, must change. Menenius continues his frightening description of Coriolanus, who "moves like an engine," who "is able to pierce a corslet with his eye, talks like a knell, and his hum is a battery"—but this is scene 4, and in scene 3 we have already watched the mechanical monster weeping before his mother.

Coriolanus in the pride of his manhood is himself, then, only a "fragment": he has taken his manhood for the whole, but it is still merely a part, representative of something much more complex. In Act V, scene 3, where Volumnia appears before him with his wife, son, and friend, that buried complexity is brought irresistibly home to Coriolanus. He tries, as he has tried all along, to "stand / As if a man were author of himself / And knew no other kin" (35); for only autogenous man could withstand Volumnia's appeal. But his own words show the futility of his effort:

> My wife comes foremost, then the honour'd mould
> Wherein this trunk was fram'd, and in her hand
> The grandchild to her blood.
>
> [22]

Coriolanus is not his own man, he cannot be: "Thou art my warrior; / I holp to frame thee," Volumnia declares (62). Earlier, Coriolanus had protested that he would only "play the man I am"; here his cue is indeed to act sternly, but he finds that, "Like a dull actor now / I have forgot my part and I am out, / Even to a full disgrace" (40). Coriolanus collapses before Volumnia's show of relationships; it is the return of the repressed, as that part of himself which he has tried to deny—the part which is still humanly contingent and still therefore a "boy"—demands recognition.

I have tried thus far to show the importance of metonymy and synecdoche to the overall scheme of *Coriolanus,* have called attention to the way in which Menenius's prototypic metonymy (his fable of the body and the belly) controls much of the play's imagery, and have shown how the figure of metonymy is related to Coriolanus's quest for simple integrity of being. There is more still which must be said about the play—but here I want to return to a question that has been left hanging: whether there is indeed a fundamental distinction to be made between metonymy and synecdoche (on the one hand) and metaphor and simile (on the other), and whether that distinction can help us to understand not only the thematic but also the stylistic nature of *Coriolanus.*

And stylistically *Coriolanus* is an oddity—a work of Shakespeare's maturity which lacks precisely those qualities of poetic expansiveness and suggestiveness characteristic of the mature Shakespeare, a work whose undeniable power is even, in part, the result of that notable lack. There is a narrowness about *Coriolanus,* but it is also a concentration, a forcefulness. "The play's style is bare," writes Wilson Knight, who goes on to describe it (with perhaps more poetic color than is appropriate) "there is here a swift channeling, an eddying, twisting, and forthward-flowing stream; ice-cold, intellectual, cold as a mountain torrent and holding something of its iron taste." [7] This unusually frigid style raises problems for critics who

7. *Imperial Theme,* p. 155.

admire quite different qualities in Shakespeare, problems implicit in A. C. Bradley's almost querulous comment (to which many other critics have given assent), "No doubt the story has a universal meaning, since the contending forces are permanent constituents of human nature; but that peculiar *imaginative* effect or atmosphere [which one associates with Shakespearean tragedy] is hardly felt." [8]

There have been various attempts to account for this lack of "atmosphere," not the least successful of which is Bradley's own: he points out that there is virtually nothing of the supernatural in the play and that there is an uncharacteristically sparse use of the pathetic fallacy. But the most rewarding analysis is by Maurice Charney, who observes that none of the characters except Menenius use "figurative language fully and naturally," and that Coriolanus himself, in his aversion to eloquence, refuses to use "language as an exploration of consciousness." The result, writes Charney, is that

> When Coriolanus does use figures of speech, he inclines to similes rather than metaphors, since they provide a simpler and more explicit form of expression. Both the vehicle and the tenor of the image are very carefully balanced and limited, usually by the connective "like" or "as" (I count ninety-three similes in the play, fifty-seven with "as" and thirty-six with "like"). The similes do not suggest new areas of meaning, but give points already stated an added force and vividness. Their function is illustrative rather than expressive.[9]

Now I have not provided a statistical analysis of the play's metonymies and synecdoches: for one thing, distinguishing

8. *A Miscellany* (London, 1929), p. 77. For similar comments about the play's style, see M. St. Clare Byrne, "Classical Coriolanus," *The National Review* 96 (1931) : 426–30; Peter Alexander, *Shakespeare's Life and Art* (London, 1939), p. 179; H. J. Oliver, "Coriolanus as Tragic Hero," *Shakespeare Quarterly* 10 (1959) : 53–60. Both Byrne and Oliver stress the "realism" of the play.

9. *Shakespeare's Roman Plays* (Cambridge, Mass., 1961), pp. 31–32.

these rhetorical figures is a far more subjective exercise than distinguishing similes; and for another, I am less interested in raw numbers than in relative prominence of effect. (Menenius's elaborately developed fable, for instance, might count as a single instance of metonymy, but its importance to the entire scheme of the play would hardly emerge from such a count.) But if I have been at all successful in showing the relevance of metonymy to the play's theme, it will not be superfluous to suggest that, despite the excellence of Charney's analysis, it is not only the prominence of simile (that narrower metaphor), but also of metonymy and synecdoche which most strikingly accounts for the play's unusual concentration of effect.

According to René Wellek and Austin Warren, "we may divide the tropes of poetry most relevantly into figures of contiguity [i.e. metonymy and synecdoche] and figures of similarity"; and Wellek and Warren go on to report "the notion that metonymy and metaphor may be the characterizing structures of two poetic types—poetry of association by contiguity, of movement within a single world of discourse, and poetry of association by comparison, joining a plurality of worlds." [10] It does not particularly matter whether we think of synecdoche as a special case of metonymy or (as Kenneth Burke suggests) of metonymy "as a special application of synecdoche." What is important is that both metonymy and synecdoche, the figures of contiguity, are confined to "movement within a single world of discourse"—in *Coriolanus,* as we have seen, the single world defined by Menenius's prototypic metonymy; while both metaphor and simile, the figures of comparison, bring together worlds ordinarily not joined, performing the work of fusion which, especially in a post-Romantic age, is more popularly considered "poetic." If this distinction is valid, the prominence of metonymy in *Coriolanus* will help us to account for the peculiarly narrow effect of the play; for whereas metaphor reaches out to broaden a play's poetic

10. *Theory of Literature,* 2d ed. (New York, 1956), pp. 183–85.

world through the addition of other worlds to it, metonymy separates, parses, even diminishes, but also clarifies, the elements of *Coriolanus*'s world.

The "notion" (as Wellek and Warren describe it) of the fundamental distinction between metonymy and metaphor has been impressively substantiated by Roman Jakobson. In his *Fundamentals of Language*, Jakobson discusses, from the linguist's point of view, the significance of various clinical investigations of aphasia, the disease characterized by loss of speech. Jakobson concludes that, although "The varieties of aphasia are numerous and diverse . . . all of them oscillate between . . . two polar types. . . . Every form of aphasic disturbance consists in some impairment, more or less severe, either of the faculty for selection and substitution or for combination and contexture." [11] In one polar type, in which the "relation of similarity" is lost, the aphasic has in effect lost the ability to use metaphor; in the other type, which affects "the relation of contiguity," the aphasic has lost the ability to use metonymy. The study of the loss of language thus reveals "the bipolar structure of language." Jakobson writes:

> The development of a discourse may take place along two different semantic lines: one topic may lead to another either through their similarity or through their contiguity. The *metaphoric* way would be the most appropriate term for the first case and the *metonymic* way for the second, since they find their most condensed expression in metaphor and metonymy respectively. . . . In normal verbal behavior both processes are continually operative, but careful observation will reveal that under the influence of a cultural pattern, personality, or verbal style, a preference is given to one of the processes over the other.[12]

In *Coriolanus* both processes are of course operative, and it need hardly be said that, in general, Shakespeare's tendency is

11. "Two Aspects of Language and Two Types of Aphasic Disturbance," in *Fundamentals of Language* (with Morris Halle) (The Hague, 1956), p. 76.
12. Ibid.

to favor the metaphoric way; but the metonymic process is strikingly prominent in *Coriolanus,* and its prominence does much to account for the uneasiness critics have felt with the play. Shakespeare is for us Coleridge's myriad-minded Shakespeare, the master of the esemplastic imagination, of the metaphoric process. Critics at home with the products of romanticism and symbolism—literary schools based, as Jakobson observes, on "the primacy of the metaphoric process"—are equally comfortable with Shakespeare. But *Coriolanus* is different; it has, as Bradley (among others) complains, "scarcely more atmosphere" than the realistic drama of Bradley's day, and realism is a method which follows "the path of contiguous relationships," of metonymy.

Shakespeare's tragedies build to a culminating ritual which contains at least the possibility that it will be a device for wonder in times to come. In this matter, too, *Coriolanus* manages to be anomalous while still bearing clearly the Shakespearean stamp. The final scene of the play, with which I will conclude this discussion, is one of the most powerful yet also one of the most disconcerting scenes in any of the plays. What disconcerts, I think, is not just the sheer brutality of Coriolanus's death, but the question of worth it raises. Is there anything in the death of Coriolanus that can make us feel that sense of an end attained, an expression perfected, which is felt in the ritualized deaths of other Shakespearean tragedies? Or does the play's lack of "imaginative effect" extend to its concluding actions, where peevishness suddenly escalates to the level of brute, irredeemable horror?

Despite its heroic panoply, Coriolanus's final entry upon the stage, "marching with drum and colours; the Commoners being with him," is in the bitterly ironic mode of *Troilus and Cressida*. It is ironic, first of all, because this procession is in Corioli instead of Rome. It is ironic, too, because (like a similar moment of stage pageantry in *Troilus*) it follows not a battle but the unexpected postponement of a battle. However relieved we may be that Coriolanus has spared Rome, there is still, dramatically, a sense of anticlimax. And it is most bitterly ironic because we have just heard the plans of Aufidius and his conspirators, and we know that this hero marching in triumph is in fact only a victim being readied for the slaughter. Under the circumstances, the cheering commoners may sound to us more like a mocking satiric chorus than a great man's deserved retinue.

It would not require a Machiavellian genius to rouse the irascible Coriolanus to a pitch where an enemy might, with some show of justification, turn violently on him. But the way in which Aufidius goes to work shows a knowledge of his man born of careful observation, and we may notice that the relationship between these two men has always had about it something of that irresolute, quasi-sexual love-hate we observed in the combatants of *Troilus and Cressida*. Aufidius looses three perfectly aimed taunts; in effect, he sums up in three dramatically spaced words the history, as we have seen it, of Coriolanus's self-defeating career. "Traitor" is the first thrust; immediately comes Coriolanus's uncomprehending protest, "Traitor! How now?"—and Aufidius answers with his next taunt:

> *Aufidius.*   Ay, traitor, *Marcius!*
> *Coriolanus.*   Marcius!
> *Aufidius.*   Ay, Marcius, Caius Marcius! Dost thou think
>   I'll grace thee with that robbery, thy stol'n name
>   Coriolanus, in Corioli?
>
>   [V.vi.87; emphasis added]

The third taunt is withheld while Aufidius provides a travestied description of how Coriolanus, "For certain drops of salt," betrayed the Volscians:

>   at his nurse's tears
> He whin'd and roar'd away your victory,
> That pages blush'd at him, and men of heart
> Look'd wond'ring each at others.
>
>   [97]

Again, it is Coriolanus's protest which brings the next, and crowning, insult:

> *Cor.*   Hears't thou, Mars?
> *Auf.*   Name not the god, thou *boy* of tears!
>   [100; emphasis added]

This quick *agon* is as tersely, perfectly managed as anything I know in Shakespeare. But what is, for our purposes, most remarkable about it—and about what follows it—is the departure it makes from the more typical tragic finales. For here it is the antagonist, Aufidius, who in his taunting recapitulation of the play's action comes closest to making (for whatever vile reasons) an effort at understanding, while Coriolanus's stuttering replies and bursts of rage prove him as essentially uncomprehending as he has been throughout the play. He does, it is true, briefly manifest a concern that his story be told aright; for one instant, at any rate, it sounds as if we are to have something structurally comparable to Hamlet's "Absent thee from felicity" or Othello's "Soft you, a word or two before you go":

> Cut me to pieces, Volsces; men and lads,
> Stain all your edges on me. 'Boy'! False hound!
> If you have writ your annals true, 'tis there
> That, like an eagle in a dove-cote, I
> Flutter'd your Volscians in Corioli.
> Alone I did it. 'Boy'!
>   [112]

But how sadly incomplete would be those annals Coriolanus wishes to be preserved! The image of the eagle in a dovecote is magnificent—but it shows no gain in insight, no development beyond the limited self-awareness Coriolanus has always shown. At the crucial instant, Coriolanus shows himself still incapable of any understanding of relationship; still he must maintain his aloneness, still reject the epithet "boy," and still, therefore, remain something less than a full man.

And if the ending of *Coriolanus* leaves us with an uneasy

sense of waste, the reason lies, I think, largely in this; for in this play, suffering does not bring to the sufferer any new understanding. The hero who from the outset would not demean himself with words still will not make that exploration of consciousness which might result in an expression to denote him truly. And what of those left behind?—for, as we have seen, the epitaphs spoken at the end contribute much to that sense of ritualized fulfillment we normally experience in Shakespeare's tragedies. The penultimate tableau—"*Draw both the Conspirators, and kils Martius, who falles, Auffidius stands on him*" (Folio reading)—is disturbing enough; but Aufidius's concluding speech is, to my mind, worse still:

> My rage is gone,
> And I am struck with sorrow. Take him up.
> Help, three o' th' chiefest soldiers; I'll be one.
> Beat thou the drum, that it speak mournfully;
> Trail your steel pikes. Though in this city he
> Hath widowed and unchilded many a one,
> Which to this hour bewail the injury,
> Yet he shall have a noble memory.
> Assist.

We could believe in Antony's "This was the noblest Roman of them all," spoken over Brutus; but Aufidius's sudden, inexplicable remorse is so hollow that it seems to me only to add insult to mortal injury. The final speech serves the practical need of clearing the stage, but its content is unearned and, like the cheers of the commoners which began the scene, is depressingly ironic. The effect is, I think, intentional, and however unusual for Shakespeare, right. For a part of the essential tragic experience is the effort to wrest an alphabet which will speak to men the wonder of life and death: Coriolanus refuses to make that effort; and though the "noble memory" the play leaves in the mind of its audience is real enough, it is (like the play's metonymic rhetoric) less conducive to imaginative expansion than the memory left by *Hamlet* or *King Lear*.

8

King Lear

In the first scene of *King Lear,* as in the first scene of *Hamlet,* the command "Speak" insistently recurs—and with the word, the need and the frustrated hope. Lear has a "darker purpose" to express: darker, because not yet known, but darker, too, in unconscious intimation of the disasters to follow. His daughters, for their part in this purpose, must also make an act of expression: an all-too-human agent this time announces the imperative to speak. Two of Lear's daughters answer with alacrity; the third, commanded to speak, finds "nothing" her only answer. But from that "nothing" comes a great deal indeed, so much that the matter and the manner of this speaking ought to be our first point of inquiry.

King Lear has been called "an immensely inclusive anthropology," [1] and the description is an excellent one. In the course of the play, Shakespeare will "anatomize"—to use a Lear-word—virtually every aspect of societal structure; only he will finally go beyond the anthropologist's proper sphere to "Consider . . . the thing itself; unaccommodated man." In Act I, Scene 1, where Lear expresses his darker purpose, we are granted an intimate glimpse at the values and meanings attached, in Lear's kingdom, to such vital transactions as paternal-filial obligations, marriage, the distribution of wealth, and political succession. Each such transaction involves exchange and acceptance—of behavior, goods, persons, power—and is essentially expressive. Like linguistic exchanges, these others presuppose "the exchange of complementary values," but in the first scene of *King Lear* complementary values are

1. Robert Heilman, *This Great Stage* (Baton Rouge, La., 1948), p. 147.

noticeably lacking. Kent's notion of the duty he owes his king is different from the king's; France and Burgundy disagree about the place of monetary exchanges in marriage; both Kent and France agree with Cordelia but disagree with Lear in their understanding of a daughter's duty to her father. Between Lear and Cordelia, most poignantly and disastrously, complementary values have ceased to exist.

Lear himself implies the need for complementary values by the ritualistic form he chooses for the enacting of his purpose. The love-trial is staged with all the pomp and symmetry which is ritual's way of setting words and gestures apart from their ordinary contexts. Both Lear's expression and the answering expressions of his daughters must be made within the pre-scribed limits of formal ceremony. Lear speaks with the voice of father and king (his royal *we,* inflated diction, and complex syntax are all necessary parts of this ritual); the daughters answer in turn, eldest to youngest. Here (in Yeats's phrase) "all's accustomed, ceremonious," dependent upon mutually accepted rules and values.

Or, at least, it *ought* to be, if Lear's purpose is to be ade-quately fulfilled. In fact, however, Lear's ritualistic mode is be-ing pressed into a service for which it is inadequate. Cordelia's answer—"I love your Majesty / According to my bond; no more nor less" (I.i.91)—is a proper ritualistic answer. It ap-peals to explicitly accepted, shared, public values; it expresses nothing new, but (as ritual must) asserts the relevance of all past, similar expressions. Yet it is not what Lear wants. The answer Lear wants to hear—personal, unique, new—is one the language of ritual cannot make. Thus even Goneril, who answers with such apparent ease, must express herself in terms which seem to confess inadequacy: she loves Lear "more than word can wield the matter" (I.i.54). Perhaps there is in Cordelia that "little faulty admixture of pride and sullenness" which Coleridge detected; [2] but before we condemn her we must realize the difficulty of her position: the one language

2. *Shakespearean Criticism,* ed. Thomas Middleton Raysor, 2d ed. (Lon-don and New York, 1960), 1 : 54.

which, through Lear's manipulation of events, it is proper for her to use, is a language that can never satisfy this insatiably desirous king.

Cordelia is called upon to speak, and to speak nothing simple. She must express and resolve paradoxes inherent in maturation and sexuality; she must, with one speech and set of gestures, pass from daughter to wife and affirm the duties proper to each state. Thus the statement she is called upon to make must be at once universally applicable (a statement of the condition she shares with other human beings) and personally applicable (a statement of Cordelia's unique condition). And the mode at her disposal is ritualistic. But ritual is only a special case of language—it is, in a sense, language calling attention to itself—and its strengths and weaknesses are those of all languages.

Words, ritual, and the other media of expression must be, by their very nature, public and shared. In the ritual Lear stages, Cordelia faces the problem, writ large, of all expression: with ordinary, common words (but now rendered even more limited by the exigencies of ritual) she must make a statement that is both ordinary and extraordinary, hers alone and yet everyone's. Language must be generally available to be expressive at all, but its very availability contains the threat that it will not be able to express anything special enough to be worth expressing. Lear's ritual for declaring love—the strategy he devises to enable speaking—fails utterly. It shows that language must somehow be redeemed from the fate inherent in its public nature, that (like the other things of men) it becomes "seared with trade; bleared, smeared with toil," and in its commonness no longer capable of expressing the particular. Lear's ritual fails, and its failure suggests that the play which contains it may be, in effect, an effort to create some more capable language.

Lear's love-trial silences the good characters and delivers up speech a captive to the wicked. Goneril's declaration of "A love that makes breath poor and speech unable" (I.i.59) is only too true: it makes "breath"—life itself—a thing of little value, and it does indeed unable speech by debasing it. In response, then, to the objection that Cordelia bows out of the contest too readily, surrendering Lear and his world to the sisters, we must observe that Goneril and Regan have already drawn deeply on the kingdom's exchequer of meaning; now, even were Cordelia to speak—to speak, that is, in the debased currency of her sisters' language—her words would not be understood. As Hamlet finds in the course of his play, so Cordelia knows initially: no amount of mere emphasis will restore meaning to a language that has for too long been in the service of unmeaning.

Lear's rejection of Cordelia's "bond"—the bond expressive of traditional values, shared beliefs, of history itself—makes it impossible for things to continue in the old way. That bond is the cornerstone of the play's society; the unimpassioned, even didactic, tones in which Cordelia spells out the terms of the bond are exactly appropriate to a matter about which there should be no doubt:

> Good my lord,
> You have begot me, bred me, lov'd me; I
> Return those duties back as are right fit,
> Obey you, love you, and most honour you.
> Why have my sisters husbands, if they say
> They love you all? Haply, when I shall wed,
> That lord whose hand must take my plight shall carry
> Half my love with him, half my care and duty.
> Sure I shall never marry like my sisters,
> To love my father all.
>
> [I.i.94]

Casting out this cornerstone, Lear tears down the rest of the building too. And here we must remember that his initial intention—"To shake all cares and business from our age," while still reserving to himself "the name, and all th' addition to a king" (I.i.38, 135)—is similarly a rejection of a "bond" (of, that is, a traditional order) and similarly suicidal. The ritual Lear stages, which ought to exhibit and reaffirm the

order of his society, contributes to the destruction of that order; and, destroying order, it silences the language that rests
upon it.

Cordelia is the first "good" character affected, but immediately we see others drawn into the pattern of disorder attendant upon Lear's breaking of the bond. As Lear rages, dis-
claiming his "paternal care, / Propinquity and property of
blood," Kent tries to interpose; he, like Cordelia, tries to
enumerate the ties of *his* bond to Lear:

> Royal Lear,
> Whom I have ever honour'd as my king,
> Lov'd as my father, as my master follow'd,
> As my great patron thought on in my prayers—
> [I.i.138]

But these are words that are no longer understood: they come
from an old order that is painfully giving way before a new.
And so Kent, following an inevitable logic, declares: "Be Kent
unmannerly / When Lear is mad. What wouldst thou do, old
man?" (144). Unmannerliness is now the appropriate mode of
discourse; Lear has rejected the bond, and thus, by his own
doing, is only an "old man" to be rudely addressed as "thou."
And as it is with the forms of language, so too with everything
else: the banished Kent continues the logic of inverted values
with his "Sith thus thou wilt appear, / Freedom lives hence,
and banishment is here" (180). Where the history that gives
meaning to language has been rejected, only the language of
paradox is meaningful.[3]

Even France, a stranger to the ritual's proceedings, is drawn
into following the new logic of reversal:

> Fairest Cordelia, that art *most rich, being poor;*
> *Most choice, forsaken; and most lov'd, despis'd!*
> Thee and thy virtues here I seize upon,
> Be it lawful *I take up what's cast away.*

3. On paradox in *Lear,* see Heilman passim, and Colie, *Paradoxia
Epidemica* (Princeton, N.J., 1966), pp. 460–80.

> Gods, gods! 'tis strange that *from their cold'st neglect*
> *My love should kindle to inflam'd respect.*
> Thy dow'rless daughter, King, thrown to my chance,
> Is queen of us, of ours, and our fair France.
> Not all the dukes of wat'rish Burgundy
> Can buy *this unpriz'd precious maid* of me.
> Bid them farewell, Cordelia, though unkind;
> *Thou losest here, a better where to find.*
>
> > [I.i.250; my italics]

Burgundy still bargains in the old language: "Give but that portion which yourself propos'd, / And here I take Cordelia by the hand" (242); but these terms have lost their validity, and (as in Christianity's new dispensation) the poor has become rich, the outcast and despised first-chosen. France's speech, concluding with "Thou losest here, a better where to find," is indeed a kind of gospel in miniature; and this is to be expected, not necessarily because Shakespeare is consciously following the Bible, but because both the New Testament and Shakespeare are exploring a similar logic of paradoxical reversal. When we come to discuss the Fool, especially, we will see that this gospel-like logic, the logic of divine paradox, is a controlling motive of the play. Following upon Lear's breaking the bond, all the normal orders are reversed; and in the relationships of children to parents, masters to servants, kings to fools and beggars, and so on, a new order will have to be created out of confusion and suffering.

In what we awkwardly call the Gloucester subplot, a similar process may be observed, of traditional order subverted, the language which rests upon it denied to a "good" character, and another language beginning to take its place. As Lear unwittingly conspires with Goneril and Regan to silence Cordelia, so Gloucester, in the thoughtlessness of his opening lines, conspires to silence Edgar. In his insouciant conversation with Kent as the play opens, Gloucester makes light of the traditional language (and values) of kinship. The bawdy jokes about Edmund's mother conceiving, about the "good sport at his making," tell us that the old man is indeed his bastard-son's father. Edmund, entering in scene 2 to announce that Nature is his goddess, treats "the plague of custom" and "the curiosity of nations" with a contempt different in degree from Gloucester's, but not in kind. Edmund reduces the traditional values of kinship to so many empty words—words without fixed meanings, but only the meanings we as individuals want to give them. "Why bastard? Wherefore base?": Edmund will define himself, choose his own words, and not accept society's evaluation. "Fine word 'legitimate'!"—but only a word, and no finer than another.

And, appropriately, Edmund sets his plot in motion with a letter: appropriately, because Gloucester, confident in the clear-seeing of his eyes, is the perfect dupe for a false set of written words; and appropriately, because Edmund is bringing it to pass (as Goneril and Regan have done) that the common language shall belong to him and not to brother Edgar. In Act II, scene 1, Edmund even has the audacity to evoke a child's "bond," just as Cordelia, in other circumstances, had done. Edmund recounts for his father a fictive scene in which he warned Edgar how

> the revenging gods
> 'Gainst parricides did all their thunders bend;
> Spoke with how manifold and strong a bond
> The child was bound to th' father.
>
> [II.i.45]

Goneril and Regan preempted the words of love from Cordelia; Edmund here preempts the words of love and duty from Edgar. And with the words come the other prizes: now Edmund can stand up (as his father says) a "loyal and natural boy," as Goneril and Regan are now the loving daughters. And now the "good" characters are left in Kent's position, forced to "borrow" "other accents," their "speech defuse"; and only when they have "raz'd [their] likeness" can they appear to carry out their "good intent" (I.iv.1 ff.). Disguise and false accents, grotesque features and alien words, are alone left the "good" characters now that Goneril, Regan, and Edmund look and speak like "honest madam's issue."

But it is Lear himself, of course, who finally suffers most from this loss of language. In Act I, scene 4, Lear begins to discover what he has brought upon himself, what it will mean to be an old king without authority, cared for by two viciously careless daughters. He has changed his identity as surely as Kent and Edgar have been forced to change theirs, but his realization of the fact comes slowly and painfully. The process begins, as it must, with the fundamental question, Who am I?

> Does any here know me? This is not Lear.
> Does Lear walk thus? speak thus? Where are his eyes?
> Either his notion weakens, or his discernings
> Are lethargied.—Ha! waking? 'Tis not so.—
> Who is it that can tell me who I am?
>
> [I.iv.225]

From this point until he is cast out into the storm upon the heath, Lear will rage and curse, sometimes beg, weep, threaten —in sum, will cast desperately about for a means of expression that will be sufficient to his pain now that the old language is proven inadequate. He calls upon gods and upon devils, prays one instant for "patience" and the next for "noble anger," speaks maledictions with a more than gothic inventiveness, and finally rushes off into the coming storm with a promise of revenge—a promise to speak and do something, at last, that will suffice:

> No, you unnatural hags,
> I will have such revenges on you both
> That all the world shall—I will do such things—
> What they are yet I know not; but they shall be
> The terrors of the earth.
>
> [II.iv.277]

Weeping is not the language Lear wants:

> You think I'll weep.
> No, I'll not weep. [*Storm and tempest.*

I have full cause of weeping; but this heart
Shall break into a hundred thousand flaws
Or ere I'll weep.

[II.iv.281]

But, as he has feared almost from the start, only one mode is
left, the last desperate means to fulfill the universal imperative
to speak: "O fool, I shall go mad!" (II.iv.285).

I shall have more to say about Lear's madness and about
the language of madness generally; but as Lear reaches that
point by stages, we too must proceed slowly. We must pause,
especially, to glance at the Fool. For in that complex character
Shakespeare has recorded, as it were, the simultaneous breaking up of an old language and the incipient beginnings of a
new. Indeed, his very title, Fool, capitalizes upon the two disparate, paradoxical meanings traditionally attached to the
word and the office, and is itself a continuation of the play's
gospel-like logic of reversed values. As Christianity is aware
both of the worldly wisdom of the fool who says in his heart
that there is no God, and the divine wisdom of the fool who
would gladly lose the world to save his soul, so the Fool in
King Lear simultaneously perceives the claims of the old order
(represented by Goneril, Regan, Cornwall, and Edmund: the
claims of worldly self-interest) and the claims of the dawning
new order (the order struggling to be born among the outcasts
on the heath). John Danby has explained the Fool's ambivalence as a conflict between head and heart: "while his heart
makes him belong to the Lear-party, and while his loyalty to
Lear himself is unshakeable, his head can only represent to
him that meaning for Reason which belongs to the party of
Edmund and the Sisters." [4] For the mode of speech born of
this double perspective—a perspective which remains double
and can give no final assent to either side—Danby uses Lear's
term "handy-dandy": a vacillating, almost hysterical balanc-

4. *Shakespeare's Doctrine of Nature* (London, 1948), p. 104. I am much
indebted to Danby's discussion. Cf. William Empson's discussion of the
ambiguities of the word *fool* in his *The Structure of Complex Words*
(New York, 1951), pp. 125–57.

ing-act between an old world and a new world still powerless to be born.

As Danby notes, one of the Fool's dramatic responsibilities is to restate matters that have been stated in other places, and especially to insist upon the sorts of absurd reversals Lear has helped to bring about. Thus, for instance, he echoes Kent's words on banishment with his own, "Why, this fellow has banish'd two on's daughters, and did the third a blessing against his will" (I.iv.100). Goneril, ironically describing one of the play's major reversal-motives, has said, "Old fools are babes again, and must be used / with checks as flatteries" (I.iii.20); and the Fool likewise insists, "thou mad'st thy daughters thy mothers" (I.iv.170).

The child/parent confusion may remind us of some of Hamlet's wordplay, and indeed the Fool's use of language shows some interesting similarities to Hamlet's "antic disposition." Like Hamlet using the word *common* to mean both Gertrude's *common* and his own, very different *common,* the Fool at once accepts the current linguistic coin and simultaneously rejects it. Because he inhabits a midway position between the old values and the incipient new (like his title, both the worldly and the unworldly), glancing in alternating perplexity at each, the Fool, like Hamlet, is able to expose intolerable social antinomies; he expresses the mutually exclusive meanings of each side of the antinomy with the one overburdened language available to him. In action (the language of gesture) the Fool exposes this tension by the conflict between what he says and what he does: while his gnomic advice to Lear is generally of a commonsense, even self-serving, nature, his loyalty to Lear expresses in action the opposite values.

And at the wholly verbal level, the Fool's intense sort of punning—his overburdening of an insufficient language—accomplishes much the same thing. His worldly-wise advice to "Let go thy hold when a great wheel runs down a hill, lest it break thy neck with following; but the great one that goes upward, let him draw thee after," is followed by the caveat, "I would have none but knaves follow it, since a fool gives it"

(II.iv.70). The meanings being loaded onto these two words, *knave* and *fool*, become clearer with the rhyme that follows:

> That sir which serves and seeks for gain,
>   And follows but for form,
> Will pack when it begins to rain,
>   And leave thee in the storm.
> But I will tarry; the fool will stay
>   And let the wise man fly.
> The knave turns fool that runs away;
>   The fool no knave, perdy.
>
> [II.iv.76]

The knave who follows the prose advice to self-seeking follows the advice of a worldly fool; the rhyme goes on to identify the worldly fool with that knave: the "wise man" who deserts his friend in a storm is a "knave" who "turns fool." But there is another sort of fool—the speaker of the rhyme—who is certainly not a "wise man" and therefore will not "fly": he is a fool in the ways of the world but by virtue of that foolishness he is "no knave, perdy."

Dr. Johnson, whose conjectural emendation of the Fool's lines would have removed some of the intricacy of the Fool's quibbling, was severe in his censure of Shakespeare's "fatal Cleopatra." Modern criticism largely rejects Johnson's esthetic judgment on that score, but I think we ought still to be able to share some of his uneasiness over the role of punning itself. The Fool quibbles, not merely because fools are given to that sort of thing, but because the language available to him is incapable of expressing his divided vision through any means but the pun. It is possible, I think, to regard many of the apparently egregious instances of quibbling in Shakespeare as comparable signs of linguistic ill-health. Hamlet puns, and (as in the case of the Fool) the result is that we are made aware of the incompatible, conflicting values of the Danish court. The craftsmen pun at the opening of *Julius Caesar,* providing a paradigm case of failed communication in a play where each man's speech is Greek to the next. And other linguistic problems are related to the problem of the pun: the equivocation (or amphibology) of the Weird Sisters is an extended form of quibbling; while the single name "Cressida" becomes a sort of pun when, in the eyes of Troilus, "This is, and is not, Cressid." In each case, the overloading of the word with conflicting meanings indicates a point of crisis; the quibble holds in and controls the conflict, but with difficulty, threatening the next stage of conflict when the tension may erupt into madness.

The Fool (joined later by Poor Tom) ushers Lear the way to that stage. He embodies the conflicts in Lear, and with his punning teaches Lear the appropriateness of, the need for, madness. And other tricks of the Fool prepare the way; his rapid-fire exchanges of fooling with Lear (in I.v.6–44, especially) have the sudden changes of subject, the apparent irrelevancies which can be explained only through the most subterranean thought processes of madness:

> *Fool.* Canst tell how an oyster makes his shell?
> *Lear.* No.
> *Fool.* Nor I neither; but I can tell why a snail has a house.
>
> [I.v.24]

Of course it is possible to discover the Fool's train of thought: both oysters and snails are object lessons in the need for self-preservation and prudence, and both reflect adversely on man's need to depend on others; but the absence of the explanatory middle terms is as significant as the rational meanings we can discover through interpretation. The connecting links are being lost, as they will be lost in Lear's madness. Speech, which earlier had been all too public a thing, is becoming a private matter, with a grammar known only to the speaker. The Fool and Lear both speak, but hardly to each other. The Fool goes on with his riddles regardless, at times eliciting Lear's attention, losing it at others; and Lear's private concerns break out with a poignant partial irrelevance:

> *Lear.* I will forget my nature. So kind a father!—Be my horses ready?
> *Fool.* Thy asses are gone about 'em. The reason why the

seven stars are no moe than seven is a pretty reason.
Lear. Because they are not eight?
Fool. Yes, indeed. Thou wouldst make a good fool.
Lear. To take't again perforce! Monster ingratitude!

[I.v. 31]

The Fool's motives in these exchanges are perhaps less important than the sheer cacophony he helps to create. There is both cruelty and kindness at work; when the Gentleman describes how the Fool "labours to out-jest / His heart-struck injuries" (III.i.16), he means, I think, both that the Fool is trying to jest Lear out of his agony and that he is outdoing Lear, egging him on, in effect, to greater agony. But whatever his intentions, and whatever the rational meanings we can discover in the exchanges of fooling, the dramatic effect is to show us language becoming inadequate to the task of joining individual men into a community of Man.

When we discover Lear on the heath (III.ii) he has become virtually incapable of hearing any voice but his own and that of the thunder. Only fitfully is he aware of those around him; but those moments of awareness are most significant, for breaking through the monomania (which Lear describes: "this tempest in my mind / Doth from my senses take all feeling else, / Save what beats there" [III.iv.12]), breaking through the obsessions and the worn-out language of invective, are the first tentative sounds of a possible new language, a language that would indeed bind man to man:

My wits begin to turn.
Come on, my boy. How dost, my boy? Art cold?
I am cold myself. Where is this straw, my fellow?
The art of our necessities is strange
That can make vile things precious. Come, your hovel.
Poor fool and knave, I have one part in my heart
That's sorry yet for thee.

[III.ii.67; and cf. III.iv.26 ff.]

But this language and the communion it creates is premature; the process of dissolution is only beginning, and Lear's wits must turn utterly before they can turn again.

With the arrival of Poor Tom on the scene, the cacophony grows worse. "Edgar, disguised as a madman," also speaks a language full of sudden turns and apparent irrelevancies. The referents of his private language are the obsessions of his private world: "Do poor Tom some charity, whom the foul fiend vexes. There could I have him now—and there—and there again—and there" (III.iv.60). Tom's language refers to Tom's world, but Lear can understand it only with reference to *his* world: "What, has his daughters brought him to this pass?" Though Kent protests, "He hath no daughters, sir," Lear knows better:

> Death, traitor! Nothing could have subdu'd nature
> To such a lowness but his unkind daughters.
> Is it the fashion that discarded fathers
> Should have thus little mercy on their flesh?
> Judicious punishment! 'twas this flesh begot
> Those pelican daughters.
>
> [III.iv.69]

Shared and accepted meanings are no longer available for rational conversation; in their place mere sound, in advance of meaning, begins to control the movement of words between men, and thus "pelican" here begets the apparent non sequitur of Tom's reply, "Pillicock sat on Pillicock-hill, / Alow, alow, loo, loo!"

This approaches the final stage in the disintegration of language. It is quibbling gone mad. And it is a stage that is, to a greater or lesser degree, at the center of many of the tragedies. Madness, or a state of mind very near to it, marks the point at which the play's society has become incapable of providing an orderly structure for the hero's experience. And the language reflects the state: whether it is Titus's self-involved rhetorical elaboration, Hamlet's intricate puns and riddles about a world deprived of certain form, Othello's acceptance of the Iago-semantic of bestial lust, Macbeth's language of temporal and physical dislocation, or Lear's full-blown mad ramblings, it is a solipsistic language controlled by a "grammar" known only to its speaker, a language that provides little mediation between characters.

The range of subject matter in Lear's mad-speech is astonishing. Here, whirling about in it, are giants and mice, kingly prerogative and tailor's work, nature, art, warfare, falconry:

> No, they cannot touch me for coining; I am the King himself. . . . Nature's above art in that respect. There's your press-money. That fellow handles his bow like a crow-keeper; draw me a clothier's yard. Look, look, a mouse! Peace, peace; this piece of toasted cheese will do't. There's my gauntlet; I'll prove it on a giant. Bring up the brown bills. O, well flown, bird! i' the clout, i' the clout— hewgh! Give the word. [IV.vi.84]

Professor Muir remarks of this passage in his Arden edition, "Lear's mad speeches have an undertone of meaning, and although he leaps from one subject to another it is often possible to see that there is a subconscious connection between them." A capable editor, like Professor Muir, can indeed provide the missing connectives for us, and they prove significant; but significant, too, is the mode of the speech itself, a mode defined by the editors of the New Cambridge edition as "ideas following each other with little more than verbal connexion." The imaginary drama Lear is playing out has a cast made up chiefly of words: the words connect, intersect, jostle each other, change places; and the meaning of the drama is largely determined by the whim of those words.

And the drama remains private. Only Lear can know the infinitely complicated rules that generate his mad language. "I will preach to thee. Mark," says Lear, and his sermon begins well enough: "When we are born, we cry that we are come / To this great stage of fools" (IV.vi.183). But immediately the discourse is shunted off on a detour created by a secondary association of sound or meaning. Perhaps (as Muir conjectures) *stage* suggests a scaffold to Lear, or perhaps he pauses to examine an imaginary hat he removes as he begins to preach; at any rate, the sermon takes the quite unexpected turn, "This a good block!" and (perhaps because *block* is associated with a hat and hence the word *felt*, or because *block* suddenly suggests a mounting-block and horses) now Lear's sermon gives way to "a delicate stratagem to shoe / A troop of horse with felt," and the wish to steal "upon these son-in-laws, / Then kill, kill, kill, kill, kill, kill!" The sermon returns upon itself to the world of Lear's private obsessions, excluding any conceivable congregation of listeners.

This madness is a nadir, but also in a sense it supports Edgar's optimistic judgment that "the worst returns to laughter." For the language of the play "imitates" one of the play's dominant actions, the breaking down and stripping away of old social forms until they are as naked as "the thing itself" and ready (possibly) for a rebirth in a new dispensation. In the Fool's language of "handy-dandy" we see the old language overloaded and tottering; in Edgar's and Lear's mad speeches we see the old language actually disintegrating. And thus the progression on the linguistic level mirrors the action of the play, where each form must first lose itself in order to find a truer self. The stormy heath over which the characters wander has its true location in the same place as Hamlet's graveyard: both are tragic gardens of plenitude where all the shapes and forms of society are dissolved back to their originals. Here, the clear-seeing man loses his eyes so that he may "look up" and see clearly for the first time; here, the king loses a crown so that he may be crowned with the flowers of the earth and discover the true meanings and limits of authority. A child leads a father over this heath. Somewhere on its borders a nameless servant (Cornwall's) discovers that "better service" has he "never done" than now to interpose his life against the wickedness of his master. Human evil reveals its bestial shape on the heath, while "mercy, pity, peace, and love," though disguised and speaking in alien tones, show always the "human form divine."

On this heath, relationships are often the virtual inverse of what normally would be expected; the gospel-like logic which began to emerge in Kent's and the Fool's paradoxical language and actions now controls the action as a whole. New relationships are being created to define such concepts as authority, service, parenthood, childhood. The modern audience of *King Lear* may see, quite properly, a similarity between this heath and that bare place with one tree where Samuel Beckett's characters wait; and they may hear a similarity between Lear's mad speeches and Lucky's speech in *Godot*. But there are important differences. Lucky's speech, like Lear's, is a cultural junk-heap; but from the fragments of Lucky's speech nothing arises to shore us up, while from out the chaos of Lear's forms-in-dissolution we can begin to discern a new order and to hear a new, saner language.[5]

Nothing escapes Lear's observation in Act IV, scene 6. The centripetal force of Lear's madness pulls to it all the shattered remains of his universe. We hear of the perversion of justice ("Thou rascal beadle, hold thy bloody hand"), of kinship relations ("Gloucester's bastard son / Was kinder to his father than my daughters / Got 'tween lawful sheets"), of sexual relations ("Let copulation thrive. . . . To't, luxury, pell-mell, for I lack soldiers"). In this vortex, false coverings are stripped away and, as Lear seeks to reveal the "unaccommodated man" in himself, he reveals the truth beneath the "lendings" of society. His perceptions are mad because they reject the normative forms that "sane" folk accept unthinkingly; but that same mad rejection finds a truth that sanity does not know:

> What, art mad? [Lear asks the blind Gloucester.] A man may see how this world goes with no eyes. Look with thine ears. See how yond justice rails upon yond simple thief. Hark, in thine ear: change places and, handy-dandy, which is the justice, which is the thief? [IV.vi.150]

5. A comparison between *Lear* and Beckett's *Endgame* is to be found in Jan Kott, *Shakespeare Our Contemporary* (London, 1965). Much of the best of what Kott has to say about "the absurd" in *Lear* was anticipated by G. Wilson Knight, "*King Lear* and the Comedy of the Grotesque," in *The Wheel of Fire*, 4th ed. revised and enlarged (London, 1949).

"Look with thine ears": a sort of *dérèglement des tous les sens* frees the organs of perception from the blinding habits of customary function, revealing to the sight of the madman-visionary the truth beneath the form. Society—its offices, names, badges, clothing—ordinarily stabilizes the "handy-dandy" that would show the justice weighing no more than the thief; but this society, with its madman-king, has lost all the badges of office and must either create its order anew or continue whirling in the vortex of madness.

Middleton Murry (anticipating the estimate implicit in some notable recent productions of the play) found an "uncontrollable despair" in *King Lear,* and these mad speeches might seem to give warrant to the evaluation.[6] But the same speeches also contain something quite different from despair. It is, no doubt, terrible to discover that "the great image of authority" masks the face of a barking cur; or that the beadle who lashes the whore "hotly lusts to use her"; that "the usurer hangs the cozener," and that "robes and furr'd gowns" hide the same vices which show "through tatter'd clothes." It is indeed a disgusting picture of universal sin, but its effect is not necessarily despair; for it may also be the beginning of a comprehensive charity which finds that "none does offend, none—I say none" (IV.vi.168). The madman, society's outcast, sees through the distinctions society takes for granted; he finds, as Hamlet did, that "we are arrant knaves all." But he finds, too, that our universal sinfulness is grounds for charity, for where no man is without sin no man may accuse another. "I'll able 'em," says Lear to the ragged offenders now that he has seen authority's image smashed and worthless.

King Lear begins with a ritual—the love-trial—which sets before us the social models of the *Lear*-universe only to expose them as unsound and ready to collapse. It begins, that is, with a failed ritual expressing, not at all what the king intended it to express, but rather the need for another, better form of

6. Murry is quoted by Kenneth Muir, Arden ed. (London, 1952), p. xlvi. Peter Brook's notable production (both stage and film), influenced by Kott's interpretations, is one which emphasizes the element of despair.

expression. The madness at the center of *King Lear* is a sort of counter-ritual to that first, failed ritual: it is all formlessness where that was all form, it asserts essential oneness where that asserted essential difference. But still it is not the adequate ritual which the tragedy is in the process of discovering. Lear in his madness can see what saner minds cannot. But the gain is matched by loss: Lear's madness, though it reaches out centripetally, pulls all it encounters into a solipsistic world where speech tends to be monologue and where sound, in default of shared meanings, controls a language that separates man from man. The madness—the mad language and the grotesque counter-ritual—is a necessary stage in the search for adequate expression, but it cannot be the end.

In *Hamlet,* as we have seen, the play-metaphor defines and controls the search for adequate expression: professional actors, as well as the unconscious actors of a hypocritical court, teach Hamlet a means to fulfill the expressive imperative through the shape of his play. In *King Lear* the play-metaphor is less visible, incorporated within a larger vision. But the image of the world-as-stage is never far off in Shakespeare, and in *King Lear* too we watch man, crawling toward death, making and completing a tragic play on "this great stage of fools." Lear's initial ritual for declaring love might be considered a first play-within-the-play; it is an abortive effort, however, with a script that gives the villains all the lines and reduces the heroine to a sort of supernumerary butt. Out of the failure of that play, another play-within-the-play is improvised: Kent and Edgar raze their likenesses and, with voice and body disguised, take to the stage of the heath to help play out the grotesque drama of the Mad King and the Blind Father.

Such histrionics, properly used, may be the great agent of truth; but we have also seen that acting is the forte of the Shakespearean villain, and that acting, improperly used, may be the means for interpolating into reality the fantasy-world of evil. Edmund, who is for the moment our case in point, belongs to the same school of acting as Iago; he "practises" upon Gloucester and Edgar as Iago does upon Othello, by staging plays which substitute for reality. The similarities between Edmund's way and Iago's was noticed by Bradley:

> The gulling of Gloster . . . recalls the gulling of Othello. Even Edmund's idea (not carried out) of making his father witness, without over-hearing, his conversation with Edgar, reproduces the idea of the passage where Othello watches Iago and Cassio talking about Bianca; and the conclusion of the temptation, where Gloster says to Edmund:
>   And of my land,
>   Loyal and natural boy, I'll work the means
>   To make thee capable,
> reminds us of Othello's last words in the scene of temptation, "Now art thou my lieutenant." [7]

Edmund's acting is of a piece with his attitude toward language: as he considers (for instance) *bastard* and *legitimate* just two fine words with no fixed meanings, so in his acting he feels free to manipulate reality or to substitute for it any piece of sheer impossibility. This worldly-wise knave looks, from one perspective, like the sane man par excellence, but his mode of acting provides a strikingly different perspective; for, despite his apparent sanity, the "plot" he stages is (like the language of the madman) solipsistic, controlled by a structure wholly fantastic, and it takes him further away from the shared community of men.

Edmund's rejection of his father's astrological determinism is a brilliant tour de force:

> This is the excellent foppery of the world, that, when we are sick in fortune, often the surfeits of our own behaviour, we make guilty of our disasters the sun, the moon, and stars; as if we were villains on necessity; fools by heavenly compulsion; knaves, thieves, and treachers, by spherical predominance; drunkards, liars, and adulterers, by an enforc'd obedience of planetary influence; and all that we are evil in, by a divine thrusting on—an

7. *Shakespearean Tragedy* (London, 1904), p. 245.

admirable evasion of whoremaster man, to lay his goat-
ish disposition on the charge of a star! My father compounded with my mother under the Dragon's tail, and
my nativity was under Ursa Major, so that it follows I am
rough and lecherous. Fut, I should have been that I am,
had the maidenliest star in the firmament twinkled on my
bastardizing. [I.ii.113]

There is great plausibility in all this, and much in its vigor
that is attractive. But it is interesting that Edmund concludes
his declaration of free will with an extended reference to the
stage. "Edgar," he has begun to say, when Edgar in fact enters;
and Edmund continues, "Pat! He comes like the catastrophe
of the old comedy. My cue is villainous melancholy, with a
sigh like Tom o' Bedlam." Free will means, to Edmund, the
right and the ability to re-create the world in whatever fantastic shapes he wishes, an ability he associates, through his
concluding references, with the art of the stage. But not *any*
stage: "old comedy" is "an allusion to the clumsy structure of
the early comedies, in which the conclusion seemed to come
by chance at the very moment it was wanted." [8] The allusion
serves nicely to suggest the quality of the drama which Edmund, because of his contempt for given reality, must con-
struct. For all the disasters his "plot" may encompass, still
there is something small, even frivolous, about it. His play will
never reach tragic proportions; rather, like the "old comedy,"
it will get itself involved in straying love-letters and bickering
women; it will dwindle to what Goneril calls "An interlude!"
(V.iii.90); and his death will be, as Albany says, "but a trifle
here" (V.iii.295), overshadowed by the tragic play which has
not contemned the conditions of the inexorably real.

The actors in that play, the tragedy on the heath, have their
roles thrust on them, partly by a necessity beyond their control; initially, the acting of parts by Kent and Edgar is an expression of the truth of their positions. And their playing,

---

8. David Nichol Smith, quoted in the New Cambridge ed. (Cambridge,
1960), p. 158.

unlike Edmund's, comprises a movement toward community
rather than solitude. They cast themselves in subsidiary roles,
taking their cues, not from self-interest but from the desire to
wait, choruslike, upon another character. Kent assumes his
disguise so that, although banished, he may "serve where [he
stands] condemn'd" and, although no longer Kent, still "be no
less than [he] seem[s]" (I.ii.5, 12). Edgar's soliloquy in Act II,
scene 3 best expresses the way in which this acting comprises a
movement toward community. The assumed role of Poor Tom
connects him intimately with the most basic conditions of
human life; his single presence joins man to man, and man to
the world he inhabits:

> Whiles I may scape
> I will preserve myself; and am bethought
> To take the basest and most poorest shape
> That ever penury in contempt of man
> Brought near to beast. My face I'll grime with filth,
> Blanket my loins, elf all my hair in knots,
> And with presented nakedness outface
> The winds and persecutions of the sky.
> The country gives me proof and precedent
> Of Bedlam beggars, who, with roaring voices,
> Strike in their numb'd and mortified bare arms
> Pins, wooden pricks, nails, sprigs of rosemary;
> And with this horrible object, from low farms,
> Poor pelting villages, sheep-cotes, and mills,
> Sometimes with lunatic bans, sometime with prayers,
> Enforce their charity. Poor Turlygod! Poor Tom!
> That's something yet. Edgar I nothing am.
>
> [II.iii.5]

Thus Edgar, as Tom, participates in the widespread action
(which Lear joins and finally leads) of stripping away whatever is "more than nature needs," the "gorgeous" clothing
"which scarcely keeps [us] warm," until through his own
"loop'd and window'd raggedness" he may "feel what wretches
feel." Edgar's acting, which is simultaneously chosen by and

thrust upon him, accommodates both freedom and necessity; it is, indeed, "the art of [his] necessities." Like an early Old Cumberland Beggar, Poor Tom enforces charity, joining the "poor pelting villages" in a community of fellow-feeling. The spectacle he stages in his single person is the antithesis of Lear's opening ritual: his disguise shows us "unaccommodated man" where the other showed man disguised—or disfigured— by false pomp; his acting points the way toward a sharing of meanings, of charity.

Edmund rejects determinism; the characters of the "good" party, on the other hand, although confused and contradictory about the controlling role of their "gods," accept—each in his own way—some higher order to which they must conform. The wide variety of theological views enunciated by the suffering characters on the heath represents (as most critics have agreed) no confusion in Shakespeare's views; rather, it is an aspect of the playwright's willingness to grant his characters the freedom to err, to learn, to find their own positions within the unknowable order. In the shattered *Lear*-universe the conceptual givens are at a minimum; rather, as Alvin Kernan has written, "In *King Lear* we seem to be present at the birth of now familiar philosophical and theological concepts, generated under the pressure of suffering and formulated by the characters in a desperate attempt to understand what they have endured." [9]

Although this process cannot be fully explained in terms of the play-metaphor, still, as in *Hamlet,* acting is a prime vehicle of discovery. Kernan shows the similarities between Edgar's deception of his blind father at "Dover Cliff" and "a morality or miracle play—with grotesque, absurd overtones— in which the poet has used his characters to set up a dramatic demonstration of an abstract idea." Kernan, goes on, however, to explain that "this is not quite correct; for it is one of the characters, Edgar, not the poet Shakespeare, who has set up this formal demonstration of the miracle of life." Edgar, according

9. "Formalism and Realism in Elizabethan Drama: The Miracles in *King Lear,*" *Renaissance Drama* 9 (1966) : 60.

to Wilson Knight, "understands his father's purgatorial destiny, and thus helps to direct it"; [10] and we might add that he *directs* it in a decidely theatrical sense, making of Gloucester's attempt at suicide an important dramatic movement within the play of *King Lear*.

The incident at "Dover Cliff," with its suggestion of a morality play within a different sort of play, is only the most explicit example of the "histrionic sensibility" at work to create a lesson or a language. Other examples are more elusive, and perhaps the best way to come at them is to recall the general impression the play leaves us with in retrospect. When we recall the central part of the play—the progress across the heath and the scene related to it on the heath's periphery—we find two central figures, Lear and Gloucester, attended by a number of assisting, commenting, almost choric figures: there are the Fool and Poor Tom, Kent, an unnamed Gentleman, the people in the French camp including a Doctor and, especially, Cordelia. Lear in his madness is virtually incommunicado, and Gloucester is bent upon ending his life at Dover Cliff; but the attendant figures guide them, when they are able, in their progress over the heath, or simply watch them and comment sympathetically when they cannot actually guide. Knight's comment about Edgar might well be extended, it seems to me, to these other figures as well: they, too, seem to help direct the "purgatorial destiny" of the chief protagonists.

The spectacle of suffering presented by Lear and Gloucester joins the attendant figures in a community of concern; it draws others to them—we recall Cornwall's servants, one of whom dies trying to prevent Gloucester's blinding, while his two fellow servants vow to "follow the old Earl" as they pray, "heaven help him" (III.vii.end)—and although there is little they can do to alleviate the suffering, still they seem to participate in what takes shape as a tragic, communal rite. The play-metaphor will not do to describe the process entirely, but however we describe it the effect is the same: suffering humanity, in-

10. *The Wheel of Fire,* p. 197.

stinctively grouping itself around its chiefly suffering representatives, is seen progressing across a desolate landscape—seeking, I would add, an expressive mode adequate to their new-found world of pain.

Bradley noticed an excessiveness about the plot of *King Lear* which he attributed, along with other realistic improbabilities, to Shakespeare's carelessness; he asks, for instance, "why does Edgar not reveal himself to his blind father, as he truly says he ought to have done?" and "why does Kent so carefully preserve his incognito till the last scene?" and why does Edmund "delay in trying to save his victims" although he must know that the delay will cost Cordelia's life? Then too, he asks, "Why in the world should Gloster, when expelled from his castle, wander painfully all the way to Dover simply in order to destroy himself?" And why, taking a still different sort of excessiveness, does Edgar, "after Gloster's attempted suicide . . . talk to [Gloucester] in the language of a gentleman, then to Oswald in his presence in broad peasant dialect, then again to Gloster in gentle language," while Gloucester "does not manifest the least surprise"? [11]

Realistically, of course, there are no answers to these question or others like them, and Bradley himself realized that we actually "regard them as almost irrelevant" in our experience of the play. But the general excessiveness of the plot, of which these improbabilities are symptomatic, is not irrelevant; it points rather, I believe, to just the sort of process I have been trying to describe. The protraction of the plot—disguises kept longer than realism demands, alien accents used where such accents are realistically irrelevant, finally even the very death of Cordelia (an excessiveness of a quite different sort)—is an aspect of Shakespeare's insistence that the characters

---

11. *Shakespearean Tragedy*, pp. 256–58. Cf. Maynard Mack, *"King Lear" in our Time* (Berkeley, Calif., 1965), who begins his discussion of the play by taking note of Bradley's objections. See also Mack's discussion of morality play aspects in *Lear*, pp. 56–63 especially. D. G. James, *The Dream of Learning* (Oxford, 1951), makes the excessiveness of plot central to his discussion of the play.

carry their tragic play through to its utmost limits, even
beyond the esthetic or logical requirement of ordinary plotting.

There is a necessity in the *Lear*-universe, a fatality, and
shocking though it may be to our sense of ordinary realism,
or to the sense we share with some of the characters of an
excessive assault upon our moral sensibilities, Shakespeare's demand upon his characters is that that necessity be served. This
is the necessity Shakespeare perceived when he created authentic tragedy out of his comico-historical sources. And at
one moment in the play we seem to have an emblem, a sort of
hypostatization, of that necessity: it is the Gentleman's description of Cordelia, and I take it as virtually a description of
the "soul" of Shakespeare's play. That this scene was omitted
from the Folio text shows how little it advances whatever there
is at this point of "realistic" plot; but its very extraneousness
invites us to read it "symbolically." Lear is on the heath, "mad
as the vex'd sea," and the French are at Dover; Kent meets the
Gentleman and catechizes him about Cordelia's reaction to
the letter describing Lear's plight:

> *Kent.*   Did your letters pierce the Queen to any demon-
>   stration of grief?
> *Gent.*   Ay, sir; she took them, read them in my presence,
> And now and then an ample tear trill'd down
> Her delicate cheek. It seem'd she was a queen
> Over her passion, who, most rebel-like,
> Sought to be king o'er her.
> *Kent.*   O, then it mov'd her.
> *Gent.*   Not to a rage; patience and sorrow strove
> Who should express her goodliest. You have seen
> Sunshine and rain at once: her smiles and tears
> Were like a better way. Those happy smilets
> That play'd on her ripe lip seem'd not to know
> What guests were in her eyes, which parted thence
> As pearls from diamonds dropp'd. In brief,

Sorrow would be a rarity most beloved
If all could so become it.
[IV.iii.10; not Folio]

The Gentleman's description seems to put Cordelia outside the tumult of the surrounding action. The beautful oxymoron she embodies at this instant—smiles and tears, sunshine and rain, patience and sorrow—is virtually the image of Shakespeare's play, pitying yet confident in the fact of its fatality. The balance of emotion, the raising of "sorrow" to "a rarity most beloved," might do well, indeed, as a description of the nature of great tragic drama generally.

But of course Cordelia does not remain outside the action. She is destroyed, and Lear is destroyed, and with an almost gratuitous cruelty or, as Empson puts it, "like a last trip-up as the clown leaves the stage." Dr. Johnson's objections cannot be lightly dismissed: "Shakespeare," he wrote, "has suffered the virtue of Cordelia to perish in a just cause, contrary to the natural ideas of justice, to the hope of the reader, and, what is yet more strange, to the faith of chronicles." [12] The frustration of the "reader's" hopes is not something which can be explained away by the fact of changing moral standards: that Shakespeare's sources provided a different conclusion is evidence that the uniquely Shakespearean catastrophe would have been shocking in his century as well as in Dr. Johnson's.

There is a challenge in Shakespeare's version, a sort of ultimate test both of the characters in the play and, incidentally, of the critic as well. The deaths of Cordelia and Lear tend to subvert or positively overthrow the comments we can make about the play up until its last moments. Wilson Knight, for instance, whose remarks about the "purgatorial" aspect of the play have been deservedly influential, concedes, "In face of the last scene any detailed commentary of purgator-

12. Empson's comment is from *Complex Words*, p. 150; Johnson's may be found in *Samuel Johnson on Shakespeare*, ed. W. K. Wimsatt, Jr. (New York, 1960), p. 97.

ial expiation, of spiritual purification, is but a limp and tinkling irrelevance." [13] My own comments about the "necessity"
in *King Lear* become similarly hollow when confronted with
the last great image of doom. But the problem must be faced.

It is a problem compounded by the fact that *King Lear* has,
in a sense, two different conclusions: a more conventionally
satisfying one first, and then the authentically, uncompromis-
ingly Shakespearean one. The play begins with the breaking
down of an old universe, signaled and hastened by the failure
of the ritual which robs Cordelia of an expressive language.
We watch that breakdown proceed in the central case of Lear
himself. Lear begins his purgatorial trial with, "Does any here
know me? This is not Lear. . . . Who is it that can tell me
who I am?" He seeks a mode of expression and completeness
where one is lacking: "I will do such things— / What they are
yet I know not; but they shall be / The terrors of the earth."
He sees dissolved every mode offered by society and is reduced
to the last solipsistic mode in default of society, madness.

But in Act IV comes Lear's awakening, and it seems to redeem all that has gone before: it seems the appropriate ending. Now Lear's question is answered; he knows who he is:
"I am a very foolish fond old man (IV.vii.60). He had lost a
child through his own blindness, but waking now he recognizes her again: "Do not laugh at me; / For, as I am a man,
I think this lady / To be my child Cordelia" (IV.vii.68). A
language—one of shared values because based on charity—
seems to have been found to effect the communion his initial
love-trial had destroyed: "You must bear with me. / Pray you
now, forget and forgive; I am old and foolish" (IV.vii. 84).

The ritual of the play's opening failed; the counter-ritual
of madness was an incomplete expression; now, finally, the
appropriate ritual seems to have been found. It matters little
that the armies of Edmund and the sisters have prevailed, for
in Act V, scene 3 Lear describes the new ritual which is the
expression he has sought:

13. *The Wheel of Fire,* p. 204.

No, no, no, no! Come, let's away to prison.
We two alone will sing like birds i' th' cage;
When thou dost ask me blessing, I'll kneel down
And ask of thee forgiveness; so we'll live,
And pray, and sing, and tell old tales, and laugh
At gilded butterflies, and hear poor rogues
Talk of court news; and we'll talk with them too—
Who loses and who wins; who's in, who's out—
And take upon's the mystery of things
As if we were God's spies; and we'll wear out
In a wall'd prison packs and sects of great ones
That ebb and flow by th' moon.

                                                    [V.iii.8]

Perhaps Lear's next line indicates why this exquisite ceremony
of mutual love is to be only wishful thinking: "Upon such
sacrifices, my Cordelia, / The gods themselves throw incense."
For Shakespeare makes *sacrifice* a harsher business than Lear
imagines. This ritual which seems to redeem the play's suffering, to offer "the long looked forward to, / Long hoped for
calm," turns out to be no end, but rather the most desolating
delusion of all.

The case of Edgar and his father is different. For them the
ending is as we hope and expect it to be. Gloucester dies de-
cently off stage, "smilingly," his greatest moment the moment
of his death: he has attained his "ripeness." Edgar, deprived
initially of an identity and the language that went with it,
also finds satisfaction within the play—justice, poetic and
otherwise. Edgar's progression through *King Lear* is almost
schematically neat. First, after his plunge to Poor Tom, "The
lowest and most dejected thing of Fortune," he speaks the language of madness. As he leads his blind father toward Dover, a
gradual transformation comes over him, which causes Gloucester to remark, "Methinks y'are better spoken" (IV.vi.9). At
one point there is apparent regression: confronted by Oswald,
that petty servant of evil, Edgar adopts the dialect of a poor

country man (IV.vi.237 ff.)—not, perhaps, because disguise is
necessary, but because the court language as Oswald speaks it
is still more truly alien to Edgar than the language of a charitable peasant.

Finally, there is the ceremonious combat with Edmund: the
nameless knight is Edgar's last disguise, and with it he wins
again his true form and language. Again, the matter is excessive from any realistic point of view; there is, strictly, no need
for all the chivalric panoply, and indeed, Goneril tells the vanquished Edmund that he was "not bound to answer / An unknown opposite" (V.iii.152). But Edgar has found his redeeming ritual. The trumpets sound, the herald announces the challenge, and Edgar appears: "Know," he says, "my name is
lost" (121). His utterance now is formal, ritualistic—an im-
personal language through which Edgar will regain his per-
sonality. Finally, after all the enforced shape-shifting, Edgar
reveals his authentic self and speaks again as Edgar:

> Let's exchange charity.
> I am no less in blood than thou art, Edmund;
> If more, the more th' hast wrong'd me.
> My name is Edgar, and thy father's son.
> The gods are just, and of our pleasant vices
> Make instruments to plague us:
> The dark and vicious place where thee he got
> Cost him his eyes.
>
> [V.iii.166]

Edgar's act of exchange in his declaration of identity is significant. But it is possible—and, in light of some of the things
I have said about the play, very tempting—to make too much
of this "charity" he offers. The speech is perfectly in character
for Edgar: pat it comes, but too pat, too neatly formulaic. And
the summary of Gloucester's history which follows that word
charity is too facile, with its conventionally irreproachable
lesson of divine tit-for-tat. "The gods are just": in a play that
has so insistently raised the difficult question of justice, Edgar's
assertion, for all the attractiveness of its confident simplicity,

cannot be allowed to stand as a sufficient summary statement. And perhaps these limitations in Edgar's perception explain why his "plot" ends as it does, while Lear's has still another scene to run. Edgar finds here a ritual appropriate to his character, and it satisfies him as well as it satisfies our expectations for him. But Lear's sufferings are not so easily rationalized as Edgar's or Gloucester's; Lear's history "can only be presented in a play like *Lear,* not in a morality play like Edgar's." [14]

What can be said about that play, with its extraordinary ending (its "second," authentic ending), so subversive of our hopes and expectations? Gloucester suffered and is rewarded; Edgar suffered and is rewarded: surely, then, Lear and Cordelia must get something for their suffering? Edgar lost and found a language; he fulfilled the expressive imperative and can even conclude the play with the injunction, "Speak what we feel, not what we ought to say." And Lear? He too lost a language, but at the end he lies dead as Cordelia, "no, no, no life!" The redeeming ritual in Lear's case, that beautifully imagined scene of a life in prison with Cordelia, is a false lead. Where, then, is the expression Lear attains?

The answer to such questions as these has often been sought by critics in some lesson or moral learned by the hero. Lear, certainly, has a great deal to learn and infinite opportunity to learn it. Would Shakespeare have withheld that lesson from him? For the sake of my own argument it would perhaps be easier if I could find that a lesson has been learned; then, the expressive language could be modeled on that lesson, a lesson which would form the basis for a new order with renovated rituals serving the deepest needs of its people. Edgar, for instance, both teaches and learns a lesson in "charity"; perhaps charity would be the new social basis, structuring society's rituals and informing society's grammar. What was lost would thus be found within the limits of the play, as Edgar loses and finds his identity within the play. Shared values, based on charity, would be available to all, and all would understand the language expressive of those values. Theme and tragic

14. Kernan, "Formalism and Realism," p. 66.

structure would thus easily, intelligibly cohere. There is, unfortunately, only one thing wrong with this attractive theory; it is, like Edgar's notion of charity, incomplete: it still fails to take into account that one intractable fact, the deaths of Lear and Cordelia.

And so, I feel, are most theories incomplete which, starting with the sense we rightly have that "tragedy records, eventually, victory rather than defeat," locate the tragic victory in some lesson the hero has learned. Robert Heilman, whose words I have just quoted, goes on to say, "The suffering in tragedy is not an end, but a product and a means; through it comes wisdom, and, if not redemption, at least a renewed grasp on the laws of redemption." [15] But faced with *King Lear's* "promis'd end / Or image of that horror" is there not something of the "tinkling irrelevance" in such talk about redemptive education? Lear and Cordelia are dead: what earthly good—since tragedy is so very deeply concerned with living and dying here on this earth—can it do the doomed hero of tragedy to get, not redemption, but "a renewed grasp on the laws of redemption"? Such spiritual didacticism might suffice in a discussion of Edgar's "plot," but *Lear* itself bursts the conventional mold and will not allow the spectacle of its suffering to be lost in the promise of an afterlife.

In these matters, of course, one weaves unsteadily over the line between literary criticism and questions of personal religious faith, and the fact that one is forced so to veer is one of the most significant aspects of the play: *Lear* will not permit the attentive spectator to suspend entirely either his disbelief or belief. For some spectators, the play will be what for them life itself is: a justification of the ways of God to man. From that Christian perspective (which in the play is essentially Edgar's), not even the deaths of Lear and Cordelia can alter the truth of the Boethian theodicy, that whatever is, is right.

But if *King Lear* is in any sense a theodicy it goes about its work in the strangest way, for as it progresses we become more, rather than less, puzzled by the presence of evil and suffering

15. *This Great Stage*, p. 32.

in a providential order. At its end we are confronted most starkly with the question a theodicy must answer, "Why should a dog, a horse, a rat, have life, / And thou [Cordelia] no breath at all?" (V.iii.306). The faithful will retain their faith, but on the basis of what the play itself presents they will have to believe *quia impossibile est*. *King Lear* neither affirms nor denies: it poses Lear's anguished question, but it refuses to offer any formulary wisdom in reply.

The conclusion Shakespeare provided for *King Lear* was unacceptable to the late seventeenth, the eighteenth, and part of the nineteenth centuries; today we scorn Nahum Tate's sentimentality and think we have learned to deal honestly with the play. But in our insistence that Lear's sufferings be transmuted into the gold of wisdom do we not substitute a sentimentality of our own? One of the play's recent editors, for instance, tells us that the Lear of the play's ending is a "regenerate Lear"; and again the regeneration is seen to be a matter of a lesson well learned: "At the beginning of Shakespeare's play, Lear is foolish. At the end he is a man who has learned wisdom. And it is an appalling intensity of suffering that has taught him this wisdom. This is a play about education." And what is it that Lear has learned in this ultimate school of hard knocks? "After much torture, mental and physical, [Lear] has come to realize (what Kent knew at the start) that he is an 'old man.' " [16] The discovery, compared to the educative torture that produced it, raises disturbing questions about the divine economy; they are questions, indeed, that Shakespeare has also insistently raised in the play, but his answers are hardly so pat.

I am not even sure that Lear has fully learned the modest lesson claimed for him. The mad Lear, raging on the heath, made profound discoveries about the nature of society; but he was mad nonetheless: his knowledge was of limited use because he remained beyond human touch. The awakened Lear, on the other hand, is able to communicate, but what he says must

16. G. I. Duthie, New Cambridge ed., pp. xx, xxviii.

raise some doubts as to the extent of his regeneracy. He says that he is old and foolish, "fourscore and upward," and that he fears he is not in his right mind. But he goes on to say to Cordelia:

> If you have poison for me I will drink it.
> I know you do not love me; for your sisters
> Have, as I do remember, done me wrong:
> You have some cause, they have not.
>
> [IV.vii.72]

The man who speaks to Cordelia of causes may recognize his daughter but he does not really know her ("No cause, no cause," is her reply, echoing, perhaps, an earlier question of Lear's: "Is there any cause in nature that makes these hard hearts?"). And in Lear's offer to drink poison, do we not see still the self-indulgent man who sought a public declaration of love in Act I?

And still we have not confronted the ending. From the point of Lear's reentrance bearing the dead Cordelia—"Howl, howl, howl, howl! O, you are men of stones!"—there is little, I believe, but wishful thinking to support the interpretation of Lear as regenerate man. Maynard Mack describes Lear in these closing moments and provides a caution against such wishful thinking:

> the man before us in the last scene—who sweeps aside Kent, rakes all who have helped him with grapeshot ("A plague upon you, murderers, traitors all, I might have saved her. . . ."), exults in the revenge he has exacted for Cordelia's death, and dies self-deceived in the thought that she still lives—this man is one of the most profoundly human figures ever created in a play; but he is not, certainly, the Platonic idea laid up in heaven, or in critical schemes, of regenerate man.[17]

17. "The Jacobean Shakespeare: Some Observations on the Construction of the Tragedies," in *Stratford-upon-Avon Studies*, vol. 1, *Jacobean Theatre*, ed. J. R. Brown and B. Harris (London, 1960), p. 38.

The image, as Mack observes, is "profoundly human," which is to say it is complex, contradictory, wider than any "critical schemes." And perhaps Lear's unregeneracy, his obstinate refusal to learn the lessons we think appropriate for him, is more exactly right than any of those hopeful lessons learned could be. For Lear, by clinging so tenaciously to the fact of his own suffering and his grief, reminds us that no mere discursive lesson drawn from the play can substitute for the play's full complexity. Wrongheaded or right, redeemed or merely human, Lear's desperate tenacity can at least warn us against the lure of the easy, comfortable answer.

So terrible are the deaths of Cordelia and Lear that, in our efforts to explain them, we are driven to more and more subtle moral and theological justifications. We insist that Lear has gained wisdom, is regenerate. Perhaps, finally, we turn to that last ambiguous line of the dying Lear—"Look on her. Look, her lips. Look there, look there!"—and comfort ourselves with the thought that what Lear sees is not a delusion but a truth beyond speech and even beyond life. But when we have come this far we may feel that the price of our explanations and justifications is the play itself: we have given up the authentic spectacle of suffering—and of compassion and ruthlessness, of goodness and evil in action—to have our discursive moral. The result, I think, should be a reflex action back—back to the play itself as the only satisfactory statement about itself. With the death of Lear, the play has wrought its device of wonder, and from it in time to come we may wrest an alphabet and begin to know its meaning.

Index